THE CARGOSPEED STORY

BRUCE PETER

ISBN 978-1-906608-89-7

The right of Bruce Peter to be identified as the author of this work has been asserted in accordance with the Copyright Act 1991.

Produced in the Isle of Man by Lily Publications Ltd. Ferry Publications is a trading name of Lily Publications Ltd.

Published in the Isle of Man by
Ferry Publications
PO Box 33
Ramsey
Isle of Man
IM99 4LP

Ferry
Publications

TITLE PAGE: A dramatic aerial view of the Blue Funnel Line (Ocean Transport and Trading) cargo liner **Menelaus** at sea; built by Mitsubishi Heavy Industries at Nagasaki, her design was typical of liner tonnage in the era of transition between general cargo and fully containerised vessels. Her considerable top-hamper of cranes limited her deadweight capacity and took up valuable space, so vessels of her type often lasted little more than a decade in the trades for which they were designed. *(Jack Brown collection)*

ABOVE: The most prestigious contract in which Cargospeed was involved was to design and manufacture a unique system of hatch covers for the famous Cunard flagship **Queen Elizabeth 2,** delivered by John Brown & Co in 1969. Here, the newly-completed liner makes a bold impression as she sails at speed towards the picture plane. *(Ferry Publications Library)*

With compliments,
Jack Brown

FOREWORD

IN the mid-1950s, my increasing awareness of the inefficient, labour-intensive and strike-prone methods involved in the loading and unloading of general cargo ships, which had scarcely changed in half a century, motivated me to ponder upon improvements. Moving small freight consignments on pallets by fork-lift trucks was becoming popular in ports handling deep-sea liner traffic while, on short coastal ferry routes, the quick turnaround benefits of roll-on, roll-off vehicle ferries were beginning to make a positive impact.

As the book will explain, these interests and observations led me to devise several plans for ferries and to help win a contract in 1961 for the family firm of George Brown & Co.(Marine) Ltd. in Greenock to build a roll-on, roll-off ferry of my design for Canadian owners (the *N.A. Comeau*). Upon visiting a Norwegian company to discuss the supply of special inflatable watertight seals for her stern door, it transpired that the same company wished to license a British firm to promote a novel design of ship's crane, and also a design of folding steel hatch covers. Agreement was reached, and a subsidiary company of George Brown & Co was established in 1962 and given the name Cargospeed Equipment Ltd.

In the mid-1960s, the growing popularity of roll-on, roll-off ferries for coastal and international car and freight traffic was accompanied by the introduction of cellular containerships for the transport of freight in standard-sized containers and the development of very large tankers and bulk carriers for the shipping of bulk cargoes. Over the ensuing period, ro-ro ferries captured nearly all short-haul European seaborne freight while container ships dominated the long-haul intercontinental deep-sea liner market.

While much of Cargospeed Equipment Ltd's output through the 1960s and '70s was for crane derricks and folding hatch covers, it was the substantial role played by Cargospeed in the development of many novel items of ro-ro access equipment – ferry doors, ramps, hoistable deck systems, etcetera – which Bruce Peter's narrative concentrates upon.

Roll-on, roll-off technology has speeded up freight transport and has had a hidden and under-recognised, but profound, effect upon culture and society. Much of the food we buy in supermarkets will have arrived in Britain by ferry but, when we go

Cargospeed's founder: the naval architect, shipbuilder, engineer and entrepreneur, Jack Brown.

shopping, few of us pause to consider the hidden technological developments in ship design and equipment making possible our contemporary experience of a consumer society. Maritime historians, meanwhile, tend to favour recording and re-assessing aspects of the story of shipbuilding over that of the ancillary supply industries, of which Cargospeed was one example. It is my earnest hope that you will find the narrative of interest.

Jack Brown
January 2015

THE CARGOSPEED STORY

IN Britain, over half of all exports are sent to European Union neighbours. In 2012, 6.8 million ro-ro freight units passed through UK ports and the logistics industry was worth 74.5 billion pounds to the British economy. In terms of tonnages shipped, the amount imported and exported on ferries was surpassed only by shipments of crude oil. For an island nation, ferries make possible our consumer culture, experienced by shoppers visiting supermarkets, malls and retail parks – as well as carrying tourists overseas on continental holidays. Yet, the development of the technologies underpinning ferry shipping are poorly understood outside the discourses of naval architecture and marine engineering. This is unfortunate because roll-on, roll-off ferries are both ingenious examples of floating technology and vital components in modern integrated transport logistics systems. Although freight ferries are at least twice as costly to build as container ships of similar capacity, they offer the great advantage of rapid turnaround and, in the contemporary shipping and logistics businesses, time is money. On high-intensity short-sea routes across the Dover Strait, ferries with around three kilometres of parking space can unload and re-load in less than 45 minutes.

The origins of roll-on, roll-off shipping can be traced back to the Railway Age in the mid-19th century, when railway companies in Britain and overseas built steam-powered train ferries to transport wagons; the Scottish-owned and built *Leviathan* of 1849, which traversed the River Forth between Granton and Burntisland was the pioneer. Ferries carrying road vehicles appeared shortly after, the Bosphorus vessels *Suhulet* and *Sahilbent* of 1872 being arguably the first of these, albeit initially transporting mainly horse-drawn traffic. It was after Henry Ford mass-produced his Model T car that a need for car ferries came about in North America. By the latter 1930s, car ownership – and growth in bus and truck traffic – had increased to such an extent that relatively large ferries with sufficiently commodious vehicle decks were built for Northern European routes as well.

During the Second World War, a British shipping entrepreneur, Colonel Frank Bustard, who had previously worked as White Star Line's passenger manager before its merger with Cunard, was placed in charge of military port logistics, firstly at Southampton and, later on, at Holyhead, Birkenhead, Liverpool and Manchester. In this role, Bustard became intrigued by the possibilities of using tank landing craft (known as LSTs – 'Landing Ship Tank') for peacetime ferry

RIGHT: British Rail's **Hengist** of 1972 powers her way across the Channel, shortly after having entered service. The vessel's career was lengthy and, as we shall see, she continues in operation today in Aegean waters, her original Cargospeed elevating platform deck system still in use. *(Bruce Peter collection)*

LEFT: British Rail's **Ailsa Princess**, built near Venice in Italy and delivered in 1971 for operation on the Stranraer-Larne route, featured Cargospeed vehicle access doors and elevating platform decks. From the early 1980s onwards, she ran on the Weymouth-Channel Islands service and eventually was sold to Greek owners. Here, she is seen off Stranraer, shortly after entering service in the early 1970s. *(Bruce Peter collection)*

operations to carry commercial vehicles. Between the war's end and 1950, he acquired five such craft to operate freight services between Tilbury and Rotterdam, Preston and Larne.

In December 1958, the Conservative Prime Minister Harold Macmillan had opened Britain's first motorway, the M6 Preston Bypass. Less than a year later, in November 1959, the M1 motorway was inaugurated between Birmingham and St Albans and, when car ownership soared, a succession of further developments was announced. Similar trends were experienced throughout Western Europe as the 1960s progressed and, once newly affluent car owners had money to spend on continental motoring holidays, or wished to buy imported consumer goods, there was an increasing need for more and bigger ferries to carry this growing trade.

In the early 1960s, most goods transported overseas from Britain to its near neighbours were carried on general cargo vessels, the loading and unloading of which took many days and a great deal of manual labour by stevedores to accomplish. Other imports and exports went by train ferry, although the lower costs of road haulage soon caused a rapid modal shift. By contrast, on a vessel carrying trucks and trailers, goods were driven ashore, straight out of the port and to their destinations without any further handling or interference. Vital to this great advance in efficiency was the development of ferries equipped with stern doors and later also with bow doors.

In Britain, Cargospeed was established in 1962, subsequently becoming one of the leading designers and suppliers of these crucial components. Indeed, as we shall see, Cargospeed became heavily involved in providing specialist equipment for many leading British and foreign ferry builders and operators – and its products were installed on some of the best-known and most well-remembered vessels. In addition, Cargospeed designed and supplied Velle cranes, steel hatch covers and other cargo-handling equipment for conventional cargo vessels.

The origins of Cargospeed can be traced back to 1900 when the shipbuilder George Brown

BELOW: Ben Line's handsome steam turbine cargo liner **Bencruachan** of 1968 operated a fast service from UK ports to the Far East. Equipped with Cargospeed Velle cranes, deck hatch covers and shell doors, she was considered state-of-the-art in the latter 1960s, but within a few years was rendered uneconomic by containerised tonnage, coupled with a steep rise in the price of fuel. Here, she is seen shortly after delivery in London Docks in the late-1960s. Soon, this busy facility would also fall into decline and, within twenty years, was redeveloped with housing and offices. *(Bruce Peter collection)*

(1860-1933) took over the Taylor & Mitchell shipyard at Greenock on the River Clyde. Previously, Brown had served his apprenticeship at Alexander Stephen & Sons' Linthouse yard, further upriver, and most recently he was assistant general manager for William Denny & Sons of Dumbarton. His wife, Sarah Steven, was from a wealthy family of brass founders, Steven & Struthers, who made propellers, portholes, telegraphs and other brass fixtures and fittings used on ships. The Stevens helped George Brown to buy the shipyard. At that time, the industrialised world was beginning to experience an economic boom that would continue until the outbreak of the First World War and so both parties must have agreed that this was an opportune moment to enter the shipbuilding industry on their own account.

Strategically, the shipyard was well located, it being slightly to the west of Greenock's Great Harbour and to the north of the Garvel ship repair dock. This meant that any vessels berthed nearby

in need of minor repairs would be likely to seek George Brown & Co.'s assistance. On the other hand, the location was very exposed to the prevailing northerly and westerly winds and on account of its windswept site, it became known locally as 'Siberia'.

From the outset, George Brown & Co. specialised in the construction of small coastal cargo and passenger vessels, soliciting orders from all around the world. The first project to come to fruition was the *Princess Beara*, a steam coaster for the Bantry Bay Steamship Company, operating services from Bantry to Castletown and Glengarriff.

The elegant steam yachts *Maretanza II* (1903, 232gt) and *Maretanza V* (1905, 279gt) were built for Sir John Denison-Pender, chairman of the Eastern Telegraph Company (now known as Cable & Wireless). Sir John enjoyed nine Edwardian summers on the latter yacht, before she was requisitioned by the British Admiralty as HMS *Zarefah* in 1914 and subsequently mined in the North Sea in 1917. Another significant order was the 527gt passenger and cargo steamer *Karatta*, completed in 1907 for the far-flung Gulf Steamship Company, operating between Port Adelaide and Kangaroo Island in southern Australia. George Brown's son, George Alfred Brown (1889-1961) sailed with the *Karatta* on her delivery voyage – a very big adventure on so small a vessel.

In 1911 the 166gt passenger steamer *Lampo* was built for the Trieste-headquartered A., G. & V. Cosulich for service along the Adriatic coast. Her hull form was found to be so efficient that she easily attained a speed of 15.5 knots on trials, well beyond the contract specification. Doubtless very satisfied with this achievement, George Brown & Co.'s naval architects re-used the same hull lines on several subsequent vessels.

At around the same time, the Yard Manager, Henry Robb, requested a shareholding in the company equal to that of George Brown. Brown, however, refused his request to become the co-owner, stating that his sons and future grandsons

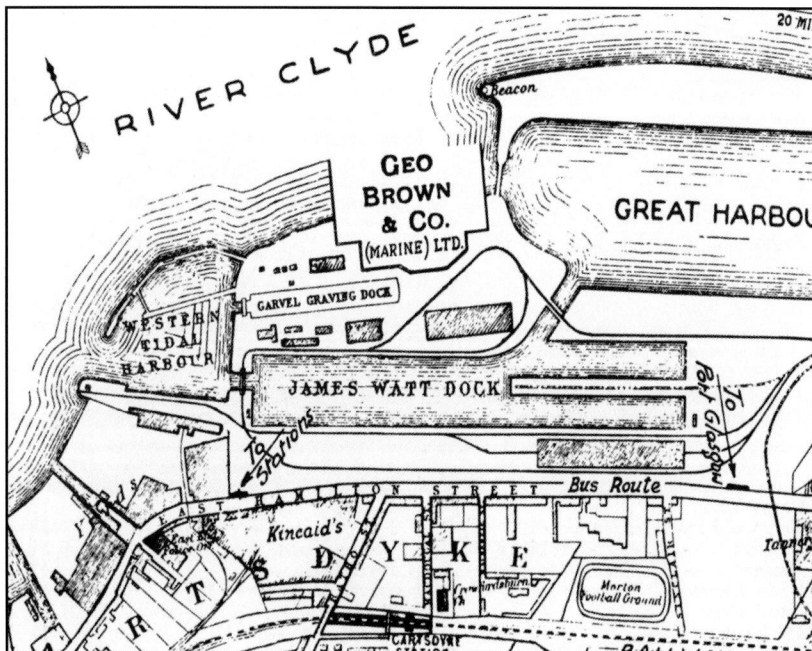

would inherit George Brown & Co. Consequently Henry Robb resigned and eventually succeeded in getting sufficient financial backing to found Henry Robb Ltd in Leith in 1918.

During the First World War, George Brown & Co. built a variety of small naval craft, such as patrol boats, minesweepers and naval trawlers. Of this Admiralty tonnage, the paddle minesweeper *Epsom*, completed in 1916, was a notable vessel.

After the First World War ended, the British Admiralty placed orders with numerous smaller shipyards around the country – including George Brown & Co. – for approximately 500 trawlers to replace a similar number lost while requisitioned for naval service as minelayers and minesweepers. Ten of these were built at Greenock and, as with the remainder of what was a very large standard class, they were given names commemorating crew who had served at the Battle of Trafalgar aboard the warships HMS *Victory* and HMS *Royal Sovereign*.

One of the type, the *Samuel Green*, was subsequently sold in 1919 when only a year old to K.L. Guinness, one of the wealthy Irish brewery family. He had her converted into a steam yacht, named the *Ocean Rover*. This had an enlarged superstructure in which to entertain privileged guests. The former fish hold became a garage in which his racing cars were stored between the rallies he attended while cruising the Mediterranean. The vessel subsequently passed through many owners, eventually becoming the property of Joseph W. Hobbs, an entrepreneurial Canadian who had set up an American-style cattle ranch in the Great Glen, just north of Fort William in Scotland; he renamed her as *Ocean Mist*. After a long spell laid up at Corpach on the Caledonian Canal, she is now a restaurant ship in Leith and is therefore a remarkable survivor from George Brown & Co.'s early years.

Britain's ultimate victory in the First World War came at a great price as a generation of young men were either killed or written off as invalids. This – and the economic cost of waging such a modern war of attrition – caused Britain to lose significant momentum, not least in naval architecture, shipbuilding and operational practices. Indeed, Britain's victory appeared to cement the pre-war *status quo* and so replacements for war losses tended to be little different from their pre-war predecessors; British coal-fired steamers with reciprocating machinery completed in 1920 were much the same as those delivered in 1910. For European commercial shipping and shipbuilding in general, the 1920s was a turbulent decade. After an initial flurry of

activity to replace war losses, there were years of stagnation. A key causal factor was the Treaty of Versailles' arguably unreasonable demands for reparations from Germany, which struggled to re-invigorate itself, suffering high unemployment, hyper-inflation and, increasingly, sharply divisive political tensions. As Germany was Europe's largest and most central country, its difficulties affected all its neighbours, including Britain.

During the 1920s, George Brown & Co. took whatever orders it could attract, be they cargo coasters, coastal tankers, tugs – or even some quite substantial tramp steamers for 'deep sea' service. Examples were the 704gt *Americano*, delivered in 1921 to Soc. Anon. Importadora y Exportadora de la Patagonia of Buenos Aires and the 2,488gt *Terneuzen*, owned by A.C. Lensen and completed in 1922. These and other projects

were very keenly priced and, in the instance of the *Terneuzen*, George Brown & Co. made a substantial loss.

Relief came from a new customer, the expansive British coastal shipping business of F.T. Everard & Co., for whom two tankers, the 522gt *Agility* and *Audacity*, were completed in 1924-25. Thereafter, the company regularly ordered new tonnage from George Brown & Co., including no fewer than 24 dry cargo coasters, measuring in the 350-700gt range. These were delivered at regular intervals between 1928 and 1940. Indeed, supplying coasters to Everard's formed the overwhelming majority of George Brown & Co.'s 1930s output, helping to tide the company through the difficult depression years that followed in the wake of the Wall Street Crash. While other shipyards struggled, George Brown & Co. actually

ABOVE: The passenger and cargo steamship *Lady Sybil*, built in 1908 for the Magdalen Islands Steamship Company in Canada. *(Jack Brown collection)*

RIGHT: The *Karatta* as she appeared following delivery in 1907 to the Adelaide Steamship Company's Gulf Steamship Company subsidiary for service to Kangaroo Island. *(Jack Brown collection)*

BELOW: Steele & Bennie's small cargo launch *Lintie*, built in 1909, passes the shipyards and warehouses of Greenock in the early-1920s. *(A. Ernest Glen)*

RIGHT: The small Adriatic coastal passenger steamer **Lampo**, completed in 1911 for the Società di Navigation Vapore La Veloce of Trieste. (*Jack Brown collection*)

prospered thanks to these contracts. After the death of the founder in 1933, the shipyard continued under the control of his son, George Alfred Brown (1889-1961). In December 1936, it was renamed George Brown & Co. (Marine) Ltd.

During the Second World War, Admiralty work once again accounted for the greater part of output. This consisted of nine 'Flower' class corvettes, one 'Castle' class corvette, one minesweeper and two 'River' class frigates – HMS *Chelmer* (1942) and HMS *Cam* (1943). In addition, three coastal tankers – the *Empire Ruby* (1941), *Empire Dweller* (1942) and *Empire Audrey* (1943) – and three cargo coasters – the *Empire Balham* (1945), *Empire Bromley* and *Empire Lewisham* (1945) – were completed. To fulfil these orders, the workforce was doubled from 250 to around 500 and, as so many men were conscripted into the forces, women were employed in manual jobs for the first and only time. Not surprisingly, bombing George Brown & Co. (Marine) Ltd was a high priority on the Luftwaffe's list of Scottish targets, but perhaps due to the compact size of its site and windswept

location, it was difficult to target accurately and so, while Greenock itself was severely bombarded, the yard only suffered minor incendiary bomb damage.

In the aftermath of the Second World War, there came a flurry of new orders. Not only did British shipping companies wish to replace lost and badly damaged tonnage, but a significant number of contracts were gained from Scandinavian owners. Ordered by the Icelandic Government, the 366gt *Herdubreid* (1947) and *Skjaldbreid* (1948) were coastal cargo vessels with refrigerated holds to carry fish. The 789gt *Teddy* (1947) was a motor coaster for the Danish ship owner Hans Svenningsen. Whereas nearly all other merchant ships built by George Brown & Co. (Marine) Ltd were designed in-house, the *Teddy* was drawn up by the well-known Copenhagen-based consulting naval architect Knud E. Hansen and so, in appearance, she looked more Scandinavian than British. Two comparatively large general cargo vessels – the 1,759gt *Jacob Kjode* and the 1,229gt *Kongdag* were delivered in 1948 to Norwegian owners, respectively Inger Jacob Kjode Rederi of Bergen and Det Sordenfjelske Dampskips-Selskap of Oslo.

In October 1948 the third generation of the Brown family, Jack Brown (born 1931) – the eventual founder of Cargospeed Equipment Ltd – commenced work at George Brown & Co. as an office boy. His job was to carry messages from his uncle, Frank Brown, who was the Production Director to the Shipyard Manager, Tommy Mclean, and to the various foremen. At that time, between

RIGHT: The remarkable twin-funnelled paddle minesweeper HMS **Epsom** of 1916; although she survived the First World War unscathed, she was decommissioned not long thereafter. (*Bruce Peter collection*)

ABOVE LEFT: The motor yacht *Giroflee* was built in 1935 for R.T.S. Maltby of Dover. *(Jack Brown collection)*

ABOVE RIGHT: The River-class frigate HMS *Cam* of 1944 was one of many examples of her type built at a variety of yards during the Second World War. *(Jack Brown collection)*

RIGHT: The motor refrigerated fish carrier *Skjaldbreid* was completed in 1948 as the second of a pair of sister ships for the Icelandic Government. *(Jack Brown collection)*

RIGHT BELOW: The Norwegian cargo motor ship *Kong Dag*, also delivered in 1948, was for Det Sordenfjelske Dampskips-Selskap of Oslo. *(Jack Brown collection)*

BOTTOM: The Danish-owned motor coaster *Teddy* was designed by Knud E. Hansen of Copenhagen and built in 1947. *(Jack Brown collection)*

ABOVE: The oil bunkering barge **Bayad** was built in 1954 for the Shell Company Ltd's refuelling operations in the anchorage off Suez. In this image, she is pictured in ballast near Greenock prior to her lengthy delivery voyage. *(Jack Brown collection)*

250 and 300 were employed and there was still a full order book.

Jack Brown, who had been enthralled by the technical details of Second World War aircraft, left temporarily in April 1949 to carry out National Service in the RAF. He was stationed at a wartime-built facility near St Helens in Lancashire. As the Nissen huts were damp and unheated, he contracted rheumatic fever and so was discharged in October. At first, he was reluctant to return to shipyard work, but his father persuaded him to re-join with the advice that 'you can either be a small cog in the big wheel of the aircraft industry, or a big cog in George Brown & Co.' Having conceded that this was indeed the case, he joined the yard's drawing office as a junior draftsman. Brown soon discovered that his analytical mind and pragmatic approach to problem solving made him ideal for a career as a naval architect and shipbuilder.

After working in the shipyard during office hours, Brown attended evening classes in naval architecture at nearby James Watt College for three years from the autumn of 1949 onwards. In

1951, he was seconded for six months to work by day at the famous hull testing tank belonging to William Denny & Bros of Dumbarton. This opportunity arose thanks to an agreement reached between his father and Sir Maurice Denny. At the tank, Brown met and made friends with its manager, Hans Volpich, one of the great post-war innovators in hydrodynamics, whom he remembers as a 'splendid fellow'. From Volpich, Brown learned a great deal about issues pertaining to wave generation and hull friction.

After his Denny interlude, Brown returned to work at George Brown & Co.'s drawing office. Although only a fourth year apprentice, in 1952 he was appointed as Chief Draughtsman. He performed in this role during university term time. During the summer holiday, however, his cousin, George S. Brown, who, as a result of completing his national service had been granted a place to study naval architecture full-time at Glasgow University – was Chief Draughtsman with Jack Brown in a subordinate role. The drawing office employed a total of seven draughtsmen, all in their late twenties or early thirties. Brown recalls

RIGHT: The **Lancashire Coast** was built in 1955 as the **Ulster Pioneer** for the Belfast Steamship Company, a subsidiary of the Coast Lines Group of Liverpool. She was one of a number of motor coastal cargo ships completed during the 1950s by George Brown & Co. for that organisation. Here, she is seen in Aberdeen harbour with large patches of red lead anti-rust paint on her topside. *(A. Ernest Glen)*

them being completely absorbed by their work, churning out plans and blueprints to enable the shipbuilding work to be carried out according to schedule.

Between 1952 and 1954 Brown additionally studied at evening classes for a Higher National Certificate in naval architecture at the Royal Technical College in Glasgow. Having achieved this, he continued there for another year, studying production engineering, which at that time was a comparatively new subject integrating business theory and manufacturing techniques to achieve better economies and efficiencies. Early on, Brown became aware that continental shipyards, built anew or extensively modernised after the Second World War, were far in advance of those on Clydeside with regard to the development of efficient production systems. As Clyde yards generally had full order books for the first decade after the war, there had been neither time nor any incentive to modernise their infrastructure and so vessels continued to be put together one plate at a time. By contrast, Swedish and West German yards had begun to prefabricate whole sections of

hull and superstructure, which were lifted in place by large cranes. (These continental yards where, of course, picking up on aspects of American assembly methods from the wartime 'Liberty' shipbuilding programme.) At least Brown succeeded in persuading his father to invest in a new Pignon tower crane, giving complete coverage of the four building berths and rendering obsolete the old derricks used hitherto.

During the first half of the 1950s, George Brown & Co. continued to forge ahead. In 1950, the 1,221gt coastal tanker *Atonality* was delivered to F&T Everard while growing patronage came from a significant new customer, the Liverpool-headquartered Coast Lines Group. The 1,220gt cargo coaster *Iberian Coast* (1950) was followed by the smaller 867gt *Netherlands Coast* (1952), the 906gt *Fife Coast* (1954), the 1,016gt *Ulster Pioneer* and the 1,203gt *Brentfield* (both 1955). The latter two were operated by Coast Lines' subsidiary companies, the Belfast Steamship Company and the Zillah Shipping Company. The *Fife Coast* was the first vessel for which Brown designed the general arrangement working solo.

ABOVE: The steam oil tanker ***Sunny***, delivered to A/S Schanches Rederi of Bergen in 1954, was the largest ship ever built by George Brown & Co. (Marine) Ltd. Here, she is shown on trials in the Firth of Clyde.

ABOVE: The launching of the ***Fife Coast*** at George Brown & Co. in 1954. *(Jack Brown collection)*

LEFT: Wm. Holyman & Sons Pty Ltd. of Launceston in Tasmania took delivery of the motor cargo vessel ***Lemana*** in 1956. The contract and a visit 'down under' by Jack Brown led to a fruitful business relationship. *(Jack Brown collection)*

RIGHT: The **Parera** of 1957 was a motor coastal cargo ship for Richardson and Co. Ltd. of Napier in New Zealand. Here, she is shown off Greenock. *(Jack Brown collection)*

RIGHT: The **Parera** of 1957 was a motor coastal cargo ship for Richardson and Co. Ltd. of Napier in New Zealand. Here, she is shown off Greenock. *(Jack Brown collection)*

BELOW: An artist's impression of the petroleum products coastal tanker **Kingennie**, built in 1958 for the Dundee, Perth and London Shipping Company. *(Jack Brown collection)*

When his hull design for the *Brentfield* was tested in model form at the National Physical Laboratory's tank, its report was exceptionally positive and so the design was re-used by George Brown & Co. for several subsequent vessels. Brown recalls that he gleaned a lot of useful information from reports published by the British Shipbuilding Research Association, which shared information about the most innovative naval architecture and shipbuilding practices.

In 1954, the yard completed its largest ever ship, the 3,155gt ocean-going steam tanker *Sunny*. Her owner was the Norwegian A/S Schanches Rederi of Bergen. Its owner, Sophus Schanche, was formerly a director of Jacob Kjode Rederi, to which George Brown & Co. had previously delivered the cargo vessel *Jacob Kjode*.

Enquiries for overseas orders came via two London shipbrokers, T.W. Tamplin & Son and H.E. Moss & Co., against which George Brown & Co. submitted tenders. From 1955 onwards, Jack Brown assisted his father with the preparation of tender documentation. Using knowledge gained from the production engineering course he attended, he developed a system of flow-charts to speed up costings and make them more accurate. These were split into three categories – steel and steel-working labour costs; wood and outfit plus labour costs, and machinery and installation costs. Logs were kept of breakdowns of costs for previous shipbuilding contracts; these were recorded on strips of paper which could be placed adjacent to each other for comparison, category by category. (In a sense, this was a

RIGHT: Lamport & Holt's small cargo liner **Siddons** was completed in 1959 for service between New York, Caribbean ports and the upper navigable reaches of the Amazon. *(Jack Brown collection)*

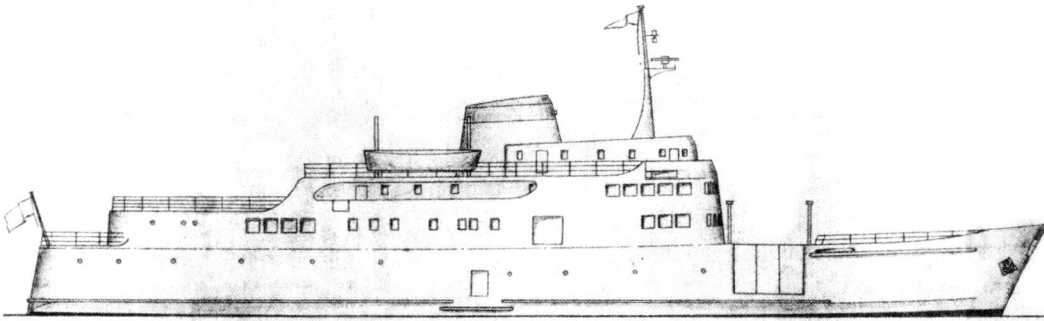

primitive manual version of the now-ubiquitous Microsoft Excel spreadsheet.)

In 1955-56 Brown prepared general arrangements for a couple of coasting vessels, the Lemana for a Tasmanian owner, Wm Holyman & Co. (Pty) Ltd, and the Parera for Richardson & Co. in New Zealand. Believing that it would be good to make personal contact with these owners in case they might place further orders, Brown asked his father to allow him to go on a world-wide business trip which also would enable him to visit as many other potential clients as possible. The initial response was negative, but Brown gave his father and uncle an ultimatum: 'Either George Brown & Co. pays half of the cost of the trip, in which case I shall return in four months, or it will be "goodbye" and maybe I'll return or maybe not.' A four-month trip was then agreed.

Brown sailed for Australia that same year on the Blue Funnel (Alfred Holt & Co.) cargo liner Jason. Due to the Suez Crisis, the voyage was re-routed via Cape Town, then across the Indian Ocean – a very rough passage through the notorious 'roaring forties'. The voyage continued to Albany in South-Western Australia, followed by a coastal leg to Port Adelaide. There, Brown found the 50-year-old George Brown & Co-built passenger and cargo steamer Karatta, still in service to Kangaroo Island. As her operation was regularly disrupted by striking stevedores (known as 'wharfies'), Brown tried to persuade her owner, the Gulf Steamship Company, that it would be advantageous to replace her with a modern roll-on, roll-off ferry. Hoping that George Brown & Co. would gain a building contract, he produced a preliminary design upon his return home but this project went no further. Some years later, however, the Gulf Steamship Company did indeed order a ro-ro vessel from a local shipyard and this entered service in 1961 as the Troubridge.

Having visited ship owners and yards in Adelaide, Brown flew to Launceston in Tasmania to meet with Keith Holyman, the managing director of Wm Holyman & Co., the future owners of the Lemana, which at that time was nearing completion at George Brown & Co.'s yard. A

friendly rapport developed with Holyman and his sons. Next, he continued to Sydney and Newcastle (New South Wales) where he attended many meetings prior to flying to Christchurch on New Zealand's South Island. This was a turbulent journey in a Skymaster 4. At Napier on the North Island, Brown was warmly welcomed by the management of the coastal shipping company Richardson & Co. for discussions concerning the Parera, which was under construction in Greenock.

From Auckland, he sailed for Vancouver on Orient Line's modern passenger liner Oronsay. He flew across Canada then headed for New York, flying home from Idlewild Airport to Prestwick in Scotland on a Scandinavian Airlines DC4.

The Parera was delivered in 1957 and the next project was for a 1,325gt cargo vessel for Christian Salveson. Named the Otra, she too was completed in 1957 using a hull form identical to that of the Brentfield. Next came the 1,169gt coastal tanker Kingennie, owned by the Dundee, Perth and London Shipping Co., followed by the 1,571gt Cantick Head for Henry & McGregor Ltd of Leith; both vessels were handed over to their owners in 1958. The Siddons of 1959 was a 1,282gt refrigerated cargo liner ordered by the Booth Steamship Company of Liverpool. She was intended to carry consignments of American ice cream from New York to Caribbean ports and general cargo all the way up the Amazon River to Iquitos in the foothills of the Andes. Her design was derived from that of an existing West German-built vessel. The 785gt cargo coaster Yorkshire Coast (1959) was unusual in that a single hatch, measuring 90 feet in length to enable steel rail to be carried, was specified. Jack Brown therefore drew the hatch first and developed the remainder of the general arrangement around it.

In 1959, George Brown & Co. tendered for three ferry orders from David MacBrayne Ltd, the state-owned provider of Hebridean shipping services. The rough design suggestion received with the enquiry featured a ro-ro elevating platform arrangement located aft of the passenger accommodation – similar to the arrangement on the recently introduced

RIGHT: The Canadian ferry **N.A. Comeau**, shown while under construction beneath the Pignon tower crane, recently installed at Jack Brown's suggestion to speed up building work. Note also the vessel's icebreaker bow form. *(Jack Brown collection)*

BELOW: A stern-quarter view of the **N.A. Comeau**, showing her rear vehicle access door – a piece of equipment the design of which led to a whole new area of business and engineering success for Jack Brown. *(Jack Brown collection)*

MIDDLE: The **N.A. Comeau**'s folding stern door in the raised position. *(Jack Brown collection)*

FAR RIGHT: Diagrams showing the effect of Seadog inflatable seals to make a watertight closure around the perimeter of a hatch or vehicle access door opening. *(Jack Brown collection)*

Caledonian Steam Packet Company's Clyde ferries *Arran*, *Bute* and *Cowal*. When visiting Vancouver Island on his world-wide trip early in 1957, Jack Brown had prepared an outline ferry design for BC Ferries, featuring an elevating platform located forward of the passenger accommodation. This feature was included by George Brown & Co. in the tender it submitted to the Scottish Office to build one of the three vessels. In a meeting with a senior government official in Edinburgh, Jack Brown learned that positioning the elevating platform system forward of the bridge would save millions of pounds in pier reconstructions in the Western Isles. Brown and his colleagues were understandably disappointed when orders for all three MacBrayne ferries with forward elevators went to Hall Russell of Aberdeen in 1960.

Shortly thereafter, George Brown & Co.

received an enquiry via a London shipbroker to build a ferry for service across the lower St Lawrence Seaway in Canada between Matane, Baie-Comeau and Godbout. The project's backers were a group of businessmen based in the Gaspe Peninsula, one of whom was involved in the forestry industry and therefore wanted a ferry to carry timber southward from his plantations on the northern side of the St Lawrence. They formed a company called Traverse Matane-Godbout Ltee (TM-G) to operate the route. Jack Brown's father was at first concerned about TM-G apparently having no technical staff. An enquiry through George Brown

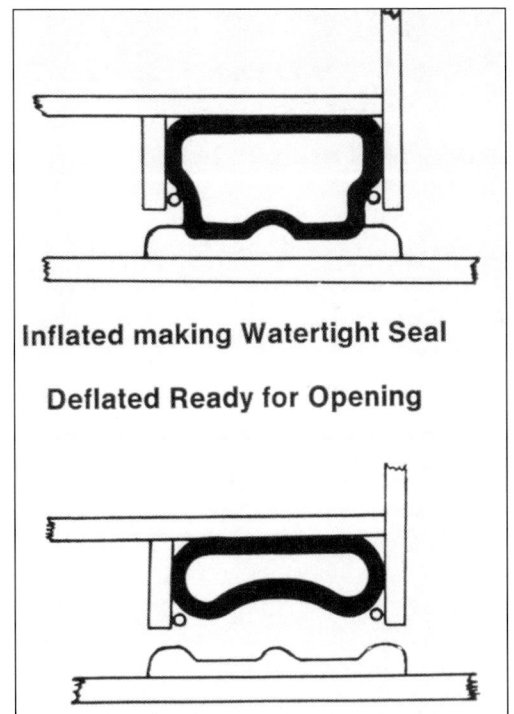

Inflated making Watertight Seal

Deflated Ready for Opening

ABOVE: The newly-completed **N.A. Comeau** on a still day in the Firth of Clyde in 1962; the ferry's modern appearance reflected well on the skills of her designer and builder. *(Jack Brown collection)*

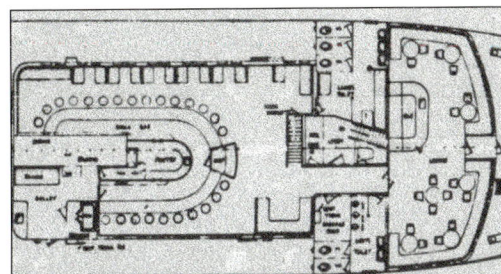

& Co.'s bank put his mind to rest when he learned that all of the directors in the company were dollar millionaires.

Jack Brown's initial design proposal was for a ferry with an open vehicle deck and stern bulwark doors, any water entering being drained through freeing ports cut in the shell plating, as was the norm in Britain for such ferries at that time. As Jack Brown already had experience of Canada, he was sent to Matane along with his uncle, Frank Brown, to negotiate. (At that time, Brown's father was too ill to travel there himself, as would have been the case under normal circumstances.)

There, the two Clydesiders found that everyone only spoke French. The Chairman of the prospective ferry company was in fact the mayor of Matane, Félix-Adrien Gauthier, who together with his fellow directors had absolutely no experience of shipping of any kind. Fortunately, his fellow directors had summoned a representative of Canadian Steamship Inspection, who was bi-lingual, to act as an advisor and translator. Nonetheless, the discussions in Matane's town hall progressed remarkably well and a contract was signed to design and build the ferry.

One week after Jack and Frank Brown returned with the ferry order, George Brown died. Some time thereafter Jack Brown's mother told him that, shortly before expiring, his father had told her how proud he was that their son had 'gone to Canada and come home with an order for a passenger ship.' (No passenger ships having been built by George Brown & Co. for more than 30 years.)

Brown designed the 1,235gt ferry, which was named *N.A. Comeau*, almost single-handedly –

LEFT VIEWS: The **N.A. Comeau's** stylish interior with a small cocktail bar, panelled in bird's eye maple, overlooking the bow and a diner amidships, providing 'over the counter' service. This was the norm on all North American ferries – but it was a feature none of George Brown & Co.'s management had previously encountered. Behind the bar is Douglas Brown, joint Managing Director Frank Brown's younger son. *(Jack Brown collection)*

TOP LEFT: A Velle 'Shipshape' crane – fitted on the cargo liner **Halifax City** – in action, demonstrating the working of the bridle system simultaneously to pay out and wind in ropes controlling a single boom. This early example has no T-bar at the end. *(Jack Brown collection)*

TOP RIGHT: A Cargospeed Velle 'Shipshape' crane on the Harrisons (Clyde) Ltd bulk carrier **Vennachar**, showing the enhanced Velle derrick design with a T-bar at the end; this enhanced the crane's balance, especially when slewed at tight angles. *(Jack Brown collection)*

and the vessel was and still remains his 'pride and joy'. He began by re-using elements of a ro-ro freight ferry he had first proposed for Keith Holyman in 1959. Helpful advice on damage stability in such vessels was gleaned from his former tutor, Professor Ian Bridge who was Head of Naval Architecture at the Royal Technical College in Glasgow. Canadian Steamship Inspection had mandated the owner to specify a fully enclosed hull design and insisted that plans for this be drawn up before a contract was signed. Given the harsh winter climate in north-eastern Canada, a semi-ice breaker bow was devised. From Brown's own experience of the

conditions there in January 1957 (-35 degrees Celsius at Dorval Airport in Montreal), substantial insulation of the passenger and crew accommodation was included in the prepared specifications. To enable three 50-ton lorry trailers carrying timber logs and other bulky items to be transported, the aft third of the vehicle deck had a raised deckhead, which stepped up astern of the passenger accommodation. Towards the bow, there was a turntable to rotate cars through 180 degrees, allowing them to drive off as they had boarded via the stern door. Carrying heavy freight vehicles towards the stern could cause trimming problems and so Brown overcame these with aft-located ballast tanks. Similar tanks were built into the forward hull, as well as fore and aft peak tanks. Ingeniously, the fitment of a powerful pump, capable of shifting 200 tons of water per hour, enabled water to be moved quickly from bow to stern and vice versa, effectively trimming the hull as heavy loads were driven on and off. This adjusted the vessel's trim twice as quickly as only pumping ballast water overboard would have done.

RIGHT: The control for a Cargospeed Velle 'Shipshape' crane, mounted on the winch platform of a cargo liner's deck; all of the crane's movements could be actuated from this single location. The left hand controls the hoist winch and both luff (derrick raise and lower) and slew (derrick to port and starboard) are controlled by the 'joystick' on the right. *(Jack Brown collection)*

VELLE SHIPSHAPE CRANE

LEFT: A Cargospeed advertising brochure cover with a photographic inset demonstrating the extent of hook coverage provided by a Velle 'Shipshape' crane; the vessel illustrated is Manchester Liners' **Manchester Renown** of 1964, built by Smiths Dock Co. Ltd of Middlesbrough. She was fitted with a bespoke variant of Velle's design by Cargospeed. Manchester Liners operated via the Manchester Ship Canal, then trans-Atlantic to the Great Lakes. *(Jack Brown collection)*

In the latter 1950s, designing roll-on, roll-off equipment of sufficient resilience to satisfy the British and North American classification societies was a relatively new discipline. The foundering in January 1953 of the Stranraer-Larne ferry *Princess Victoria* – when waves breached her stern bulwark doors, causing the vehicle deck to flood at a faster rate than the freeing ports could drain water away – was a tragedy still fresh in naval architects' minds. Brown got good advice

ABOVE: The splendid Bristol City Line motor cargo ship **Halifax City** on trials in the Firth of Forth in 1964 shortly after completion by Burntisland Shipbuilding Ltd in Fife. All of her forward hatches are serviced by Cargospeed Velle 'Shipshape' cranes. *(Jack Brown collection)*

from Bob Lockhart, Lloyd's of London's Senior Naval Architect dealing with the approval of hulls and structures.

To achieve a reliably watertight stern door, Brown became intrigued by the possibilities offered by a type of pneumatic seal marketed as 'Seadog' by an Oslo-based supplier of specialist maritime equipment, Finn Tveten & Co. This consisted of a neoprene inflatable tube housed in a steel channel around the perimeter of a hatch or door and a corresponding shallow steel ridge around the doorframe. Once inflated, the neoprene tube formed a watertight seal.

When preparing the unsuccessful tender for the Scottish Office on behalf of David MacBrayne, contact was made with Keelavite Hydraulics Ltd to quote for a hydraulic system to operate a vehicle lift. Recalling the excellent advice received from Keelavite's engineers, the hydraulic power pack and operating cylinder for the stern door installed on the *N.A. Comeau* were ordered from the company. This system made use of the 'Keelaring' hydraulic pipe coupling. It featured an O-ring seal, as opposed to a metal ring cutting into the pipe which was the norm at that time. A simple demonstration of a 'Keelaring' coupling

RIGHT & BELOW: Another product of Burntisland Shipbuilding Ltd, the Houlder Bros cargo liner **Tenbury** was delivered in 1965 and had both Velle 'Shipshape' cranes and an extensive array of Velle flush 'tween deck hatch covers. The left-hand and centre views show the 'tween deck covers stowed at the end of a hatch way and, right, the completely flush deck surface of the hatch cover in the closed position, thereby allowing cargo consignments to be moved all over the deck on forklift trucks. *(Jack Brown collection)*

with the securing nut screwed hand-tight, then sustaining 3,000 psi (pounds per square inch) or 210 bars pressure, was enough to convince Brown of its effectiveness. Brown subsequently specified 'Keelaring' couplings for the hydraulic systems activating the doors, hatches and ramps on over a hundred subsequent Cargospeed contracts.

Externally, the N.A. Comeau was a handsome ferry of up-to-date appearance, Brown taking particular pride in achieving harmonious details in the plated-in bulwarks, the curving forward superstructure, raked tripod masts and tapered funnel. Some inspiration for the internal passenger accommodation details came from suggestions made by a friendly naval architect working at Greenock Dockyard Ltd. The N.A. Comeau's design was very successful and the vessel enjoyed a 25-year-long career on the St Lawrence before being converted in 1988 as a cruise ship which operated under several names in Caribbean waters until 1994. She was then moved to permanent mooring in Hastings, Port Philip Bay in Australia as a floating conference centre named Xanadu.

When Brown visited Finn Tveten to discuss how 'Seadog' seals might be utilised in a ferry stern door, he found a good rapport and discovered that Tveten also possessed a contract to market Velle 'Shipshape' crane derricks and Velle steel hatch covers for cargo vessels. These were inventions of Captain Edvard H. Velle, formerly a master of the Norwegian America Line's trans-Atlantic passenger vessels. After a lengthy and distinguished career at sea, the retired Captain had used his accumulated knowledge to design a new and considerably more effective crane type than the traditional 'union purchase' twin derricks hitherto fitted on most cargo vessels. Velle's design had a single mast with a Y-shaped head from which ropes connected to a bridle, which was attached to the end of the boom. On the winch platform, two double-barrel winches enabled two sets of fall wires to be paid out and wound in simultaneously

TOP RIGHT: A Cargospeed Velle Shipshape crane erected on a U.S.Navy barge for the unshipping of periscopes from submarines afloat. This crane featured Jack Brown's three point suspension arrangement for maximum stability of the load hook. (Jack Brown collection)

so that the boom could be raised, lowered and swung quickly. Other advantages were that the boom had far greater stability, there was less clutter on deck due to the lack of guy ropes and one man could control all movements from a single console, meaning a significant saving of labour.

In Norway, Velle hatch cover systems were designed by Velle Systemer A/S, a company in Moss on the Oslofjord, which was separate from Finn Tveten's Oslo-based sales business. As Tveten's UK sales agent was failing to make an impact in the potentially lucrative British market, Tveten discussed with Jack Brown the possibility of the latter taking over this activity – and also manufacturing the cranes and hatch covers under licence at George Brown & Co.'s yard.

Brown's Norwegian contact was to prove invaluable for George Brown & Co. The early 1960s turned out to be a fallow period for shipbuilding in the UK and so it was necessary for

LEFT: The boom for a Cargospeed Velle crane awaiting transporting from George Brown & Co. (Marine) Ltd's Garvel shipyard, demonstrating the large size of such fabrications which, however, look trivial in scale once installed on a ship. (Jack Brown collection)

RIGHT: A model of Jack Brown's first patent design – a 'finger platform' for the rapid loading of palletised cargoes by forklift trucks; when extended from vertical to over-side, truck drivers both on the quay and aboard the vessel had sight of each other between the fingers. *(Jack Brown collection)*

the company to diversify into other areas. Frantic international construction activity since 1945 had almost entirely renewed the world's merchant fleet – and now foreign yards utilising up-to-date facilities, more efficient production techniques and with more progressive labour relations were providing tough competition for such orders as were available. In the 1958-1961 period, George Brown & Co. tendered unsuccessfully for 140 contracts but won only two – to build the tug *Brigadier* for Steel & Bennie and a grab hopper dredger named the *Kakuluwa* (which appropriately translates as 'crab') for the Colombo Port Commission.

Jack Brown recalls that, in Clydeside shipyards, there were no fewer than 17 trade unions representing different trades with precisely defined demarcations between each. He recalls a typical dispute of the era that took place at the Charles Connell & Co. shipyard. It involved joiners and upholsterers and the issue was whether the former or the latter should be responsible for fitting brass non-slip treads to ship's staircases. Its resolution was that upholsterers should do the job – but with an equal number of joiners standing by doing nothing. While George Brown & Co.'s industrial relations were better than at most other Clyde yards, it was nonetheless bound by decisions arrived at by collective bargaining between the shipyards' managements and the unions. The former increasingly came to the unfortunate conclusion that, faced with West German, Scandinavian and Japanese competition for orders, there was little future for building vessels on the Clyde.

Between 1962 and 1964, no fewer than nine Clyde yards ceased shipbuilding operations, including such famous names as Wm Denny & Bros of Dumbarton and Harland & Wolff in Govan. George Brown & Co. gained just two further orders after the *N.A. Comeau* for new ships, 1,985gt *Kinnaird Head* for Henry & McGregor and a twin-screw tugboat, the 275gt *Vasabha*, again for the Colombo Port Commission. Once they were fulfilled in 1962-63, shipbuilding operations ceased. Jack Brown's uncle, Frank, who was George Brown & Co.'s 42 per cent shareholder, wanted to liquidate the company – but Jack, with

58 per cent following his father's demise, decided to continue.

In the meantime, the yard began to manufacture Velle 'Shipshape' cranes for cargo vessels under construction at other yards elsewhere in the UK for a variety of British and overseas owners. To do so, in February 1962, Jack Brown established Cargospeed Equipment Ltd specifically to design and market Velle cranes and hatch covers under licence. Brown was its Managing Director and principal designer, being assisted in the latter role by Ron Ballantyne, whom Brown recalls was a very talented mechanical engineer. Previously, Ballantyne had been employed by Wm Denny & Bros, where he had produced unrealised designs for hovercraft, amongst other projects. The cranes and hatches Cargospeed offered would ideally be manufactured by George Brown & Co., which remained as a separate company, or if necessary by the shipyards building the vessels to which they would be fitted.

From a marketing perspective, the name 'Cargospeed' was a good choice, clearly signalling to ship owners the company's intention of helping them to become more efficient. In the early 1960s, a typical general cargo liner spent at least half of its time alongside as loading and unloading was a painstakingly slow and labour-intensive process. As Jack Brown observes, ships have an opportunity to earn money only when they are sailing. Tied up at a quay, a vessel becomes an expensive warehouse for which the owner pays handsomely. Because it offered the potential for very short port turnarounds, roll-on, roll-off was the best cargo handling method in Brown's opinion, but still there was scope greatly to improve the efficiency of conventional 'union-purchase' cargo-handling and so, for the time being, Velle 'Shipshape' cranes and Velle hatch cover systems had roles to play.

Although from the outset Cargospeed used George Brown & Co.'s production facilities, at the insistence of Frank Brown, who wanted nothing to do with it, offices were leased in Grey Place in Greenock until Frank's retirement in 1963. Subsequently, thanks to Jack Brown's fertile engineering imagination, Cargospeed developed

ABOVE: The geared bulk carrier **Middlesex Trader**, built by Austin & Pickersgill Ltd of Sunderland and delivered in 1963 to Trader Navigation, was the first vessel fitted with Cargospeed Velle folding steel hatch covers. *(Jack Brown collection)*

a range of state-of-the-art cargo handling and access equipment, including non-Velle steel hatch covers for freighters and bulk carriers and hull doors, ramps and hoistable platform decks for ferries.

In entering this market, Cargospeed would be competing with a small number of established businesses. The best known of these was MacGregor. It was the creation of two engineers of Scottish origin, the brothers Robert and Joseph MacGregor, who lived in Whitley Bay in the North-East of England. During the latter 1920s, they had first designed steel hatch covers for colliers, bringing coal coastwise from the Tyne to London. Consisting of five articulated leaves, these stowed neatly at the end of each hatch. Hitherto, vessels' deck crews had enclosed hatches with steel beams, timber and canvas – a procedure requiring many hours to complete, whereas MacGregor's hatch covers could be closed in minutes. The Great Depression put a temporary halt to the spread of this significant innovation and it was not until 1937 that the brothers actually established MacGregor & Company. After the

Second World War, MacGregor entered into a joint arrangement with the French company, Comarain, whose head, Henri Kummerman, began an aggressive programme of expansion. Thus, by the 1960s, MacGregor was the market leader in the supply of watertight hatches for

LEFT: Side-rolling hatch covers on **Vardefjell**, as described overleaf. *(Jack Brown collection)*

LEFT: A Cargospeed Velle folding hatch cover battened down and made watertight by quick-acting cleats; a row of eye-bolts is attached to the hatch frame and to the outer edges of the cover. By lowering the levers on the hatch frame, the bolts are tightened and a watertight seal is achieved. *(Jack Brown collection)*

TOP: The *St Benedict* was the last of a class of five fish factory trawlers constructed between 1964 and 1973. Equipped with Cargospeed's own design of hydraulically operated hatch cover and stern gates, the vessel was by Ferguson Bros Ltd of Port Glasgow for Thomas Hamling & Co. Ltd. *(Bruce Peter collection)*

TOP LEFT & RIGHT: The *St Benedict*'s stern gates opened to allow the fish net to be dragged up the stern ramp. A flush hatch in the deck raised, enabling the fish to be emptied into the factory deck. *(Jack Brown collection)*

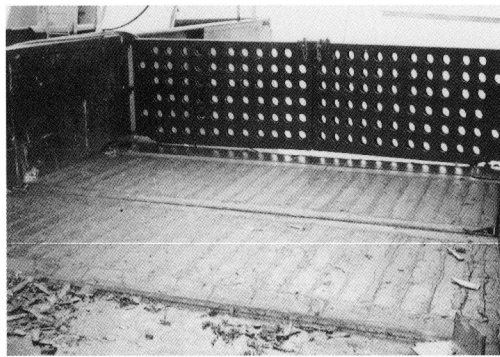

LOWER MIDDLE: The Norwegian Olsen & Uglestad A/S-owned 11,991gt oil tanker *Vardefjell* was converted in 1968 by Firth of Clyde Drydock Co. Ltd into an oil-bulk-ore (OBO) carrier, equipped with hydraulically powered, side-rolling, double-skin Cargospeed Velle hatch covers. *(Jack Brown collection)*

BOTTOM LEFT & RIGHT: The 1,573gt trawler *Othello* was the first of a class of four built in 1966-67 by Yarrow & Co. Ltd in Glasgow for Hellyer Bros Ltd (Associated Fisheries). The left-hand image shows her hydraulically powered stern gates with port and starboard fish hatches, actuated by Konex hinges. The right-hand image shows a hatch in the process of opening. *(Jack Brown*

ships and it was also making strides in developing equipment for roll-on, roll-off ferries. A second supplier of steel hatch covers was Cargocover, founded in 1955 and, two years thereafter, a third entrant was the Finnish company Oy Navire AB, established in 1957. Thus, with the establishment of Cargospeed in 1962, there were at least four potential competitors designing and manufacturing steel hatch covers for ships.

Even before Cargospeed was established, Jack Brown had applied his mind to designing systems to enhance cargo handling efficiency. Containerisation was still in its infancy and most British liner companies remained committed to general cargo vessels equipped with union-purchase derricks. In 1958, Brown had the idea of a folding platform at shelter deck level to enable consignments of pallets to be handled by forklift

LEFT: The General Steam Navigation Co. Ltd's 584gt North Sea cargo vessel *Avocet* of 1965 which, with her sister, the *Albatross*, was fully equipped with Cargospeed Velle hatch covers. The vessels were built by John Lewis & Sons Ltd of Aberdeen. *(Jack Brown collection)*

CENTRE LEFT: The weather deck hatch covers on the *Avocet* in the open position. *(Jack Brown collection)*

CENTRE RIGHT: The folding flush 'tween deck hatch covers with no fewer than six hinged panels stowed at one end of the hatch, an unusual solution necessitated by the restricted 'tween deck height. *(Jack Brown collection)*

LOWER LEFT & RIGHT: A 90-degree Konex hinge at a hatch end at weather deck height (left) and two Konex hinges with opposing actions, giving a 180-degree motion at the joint between two hatch panels. *(Jack Brown collection)*

trucks both ashore and on board. Unbeknown to him, however, a Norwegian engineer called Erik Heirung had a similar idea, which he developed jointly with MacGregor, initially testing it on a coastal cargo vessel named the *Verma*. While Heirung advocated shipboard forklift trucks passing palettes to ones on the quayside, Brown's solution was more sophisticated as he developed a fold-out platform system, consisting of a series of steel forks forming a shelf. Palletised consignments could be placed on this shelf, from which they could be collected. Brown marketed his concept as a 'finger platform' but none of the British liner companies whom he approached to

try out his design was interested. Eventually, in the second half of the 1960s, some belatedly invested in side doors through which palletised cargoes could be handled over a fold-out platform by forklift trucks. By then, thanks to Heirung, palletised handling of so-called 'unit loads' was standard practice on nearly all Scandinavian-owned cargo liners.

Cargospeed's first contract was to supply designs and components for hatch covers for the 13,461dw bulk carrier *Middlesex Trader*, under construction at Austin & Pickersgill's shipyard on the River Tees for delivery to Trader Navigation Co. in 1963. Austin & Pickersgill fabricated the hatch covers, using Cargospeed plans derived from Velle's design. The hinges, rollers, securing cleats and other fittings were made by George Brown & Co. while Velle supplied twin-chamber neoprene packings to ensure the hatches' water-tightness.

In 1964, Cargospeed won its first contract to design ro-ro ferry equipment. That year, British Railways placed orders for two new steam turbine-powered car ferries, one to be named

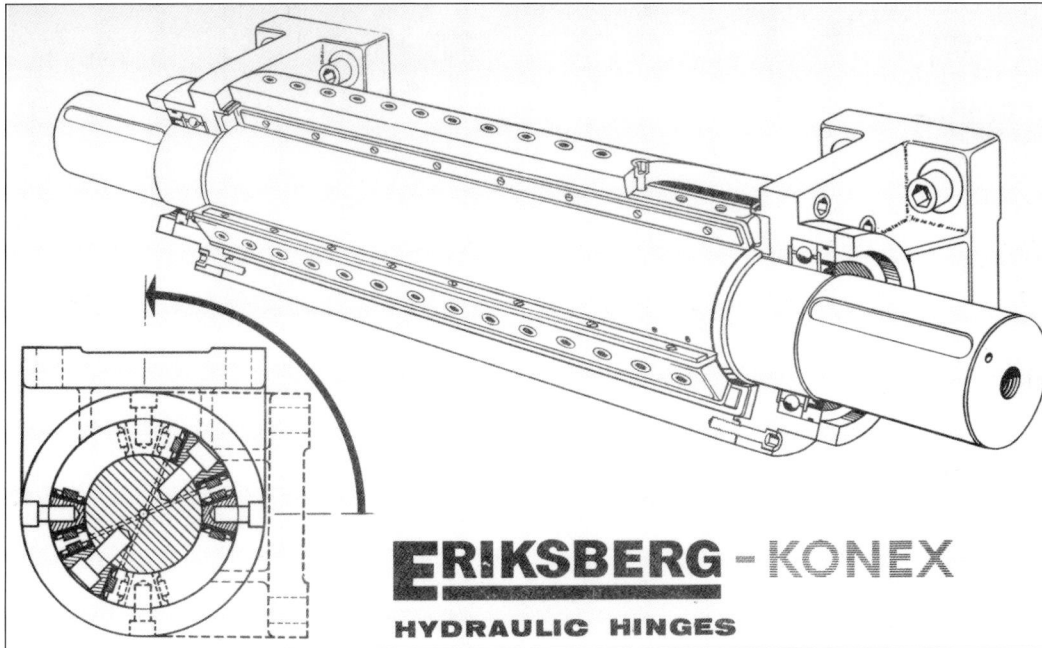

ERIKSBERG - KONEX
HYDRAULIC HINGES

BELOW: The hinged bow doors on the *Sir Bedivere* and her Cargospeed-equipped sisters were mounted on short arms so that they 'unplugged' from the shell plating before opening outward. It was therefore possible to achieve a neat fit as there was no need to leave a gap where the doors' edges met the hull shell. *(Jack Brown collection)*

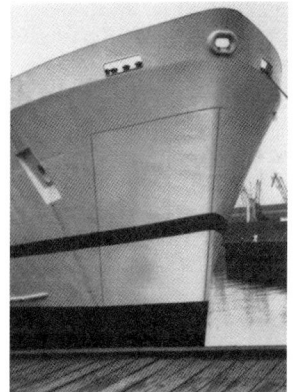

BELOW: The landing ship *Sir Bedivere*, completed in 1967 by Hawthorn Leslie Ltd of Newcastle, was one of a series fitted with Cargospeed hinged bow doors and ramp and also Cargospeed davits to launch life-rafts. *(Jack Brown collection)*

Holyhead Ferry I for the Holyhead-Dun Laoghaire route across the Irish Sea and the other to be called *Dover* for the short, high-intensity Dover-Calais service. The main contracts and subcontracts for these vessels were subject to competitive tender and so orders were placed with two shipyards. Hawthorn Leslie & Co. of Hebburn was to construct the former while Swan Hunter & Co. of Wallsend, which faced it across the River Tyne, would build the latter. The contracts for ro-ro equipment also went to different providers, Cargospeed supplying the stern door, mezzanine deck access ramps and associated equipment for the *Holyhead Ferry I* (all of which were manufactured by George Brown & Co.) while MacGregor would deliver a similar range of items for the *Dover*. The *Holyhead Ferry I* project brought Jack Brown into contact with British Rail's charming and talented in-house naval architects Tony Rogan and Don Ripley, with whom he went on to enjoy a fruitful working relationship

during the ensuing 15 years.

Although very similar in terms of external appearance, the two vessels had significant variations in internal layout, the *Holyhead Ferry I* having a larger passenger accommodation, filling the midships part of the hull's upper deck level, while the *Dover* had clear space for vehicles throughout. On both vessels, a fixed mezzanine deck was installed in the forward part of the hull, allowing cars to be parked there on two levels. They were likewise stern-loaders with a turntable for cars at the bow.

The *Holyhead Ferry I*'s stern door was located some way inboard of the stern shell plating and belting and it hinged upwards and aft. It was mounted on a KONEX hinge, a powerful but reliable hydraulic actuator discovered by Jack Brown when he visited the Eriksberg shipyard in Gothenburg, which owned a manufacturing patent. The KONEX design was robust and efficient, providing a maximum rotation of 90

RIGHT: Cargospeed's davit design for Royal Fleet Auxiliary landing craft in action, showing how the frame was swung outboard of the vessel's hull. This enabled a rubber life-raft to be inflated quickly, filled with men and lowered onto the sea then released. This equipment was used subsequently in hostile conditions during the Falklands War in 1982 when the RFA **Sir Galahad** came under missile attack. (*Jack Brown collection*)

LOWER LEFT AND BOTTOM: The ro-ro freighter **Seaway Princess** was built by the Hong Kong & Whampoa Dockyard Co. of Hong Kong and delivered in 1966 to the Northern Steamship Company of New Zealand. Cargospeed supplied the stern door (a hinged design, shown here in its open position) but had wanted to provide more complex access equipment for the vessel, a model of which is shown below right. (*Jack Brown collection*)

degrees, or 180 degrees by using twin hinges rotating in opposite directions on a common shaft. As with the *N.A. Comeau*, Seadog inflatable seals were fitted around the door's perimeter to keep it watertight. Brown recalls that there was great delight at the shipyard on the day when the *Holyhead Ferry I*'s stern door was tested – Hawthorn Leslie & Co.'s workers applauded and cheered as the door lifted smoothly on its KONEX

hinge while the employees of Swan Hunter & Co. on the opposite bank looked on in silence.

While the *Holyhead Ferry I* project was commencing, early in 1964, Cargospeed won a contract to supply weather deck and 'tween deck hatch covers for an Icelandic 2,361gt refrigerated cargo vessel shortly to be constructed by Grangemouth Dockyard Co. Ltd. Brown flew to Reykjavik to meet the ship owner H.F. Jocklar, bringing with him cine films not only showing Cargospeed hatch covers in use, but also the operation of Velle cranes. Jocklar was enthused about both and wanted to know if there was any way that Velle cranes could be made to fit his forthcoming ship. Brown worked through the night to draw plans (due to the midnight sun, there was daylight lasting 24 hours). When Brown returned to Scotland, he received a phone call from Grangemouth Dockyard's Managing Director, who began with 'Jack – what have you been doing? You've got orders for hatch covers AND

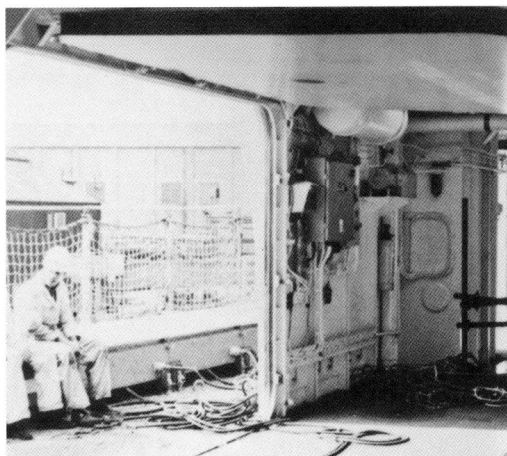

LEFT: One of the Cargospeed access doors on the MOD stores support ships *Lyness*, *Stromness* and *Tarbatness* is tested at Swan Hunter's Wallsend shipyard in 1967. *(Jack Brown collection)*

RIGHT: A Hydromite hydrolic power pack of the type used to open and close the doors on these vessels. *(Jack Brown collection)*

BOTTOM LEFT: One of the side doors, activated by Konex hinges, in the closed position. *(Jack Brown collection)*

Sir Percivale, ordered from Hawthorn Leslie Ltd on the Tyne. Already, a prototype for the class, named *Sir Lancelot*, had been completed by Fairfield Shipbuilding & Engineering Ltd with equivalent equipment supplied by MacGregor. Operated on behalf of the Royal Fleet Auxiliary Service by a P&O Group subsidiary, the British India Steam Navigation Company Ltd, the craft were designed to carry 400 troops each, as well as tanks, munitions and other military hardware. In order to land helicopters, the weather deck needed to remain unobstructed by lifeboat davits, or any other cluttering deck equipment. Cargospeed therefore developed a special type of davit, lowered by winch and locked in place. Un-inflated rafts were hooked to these then inflated (for filling with men) prior to being lowered into the water, after which the hooks automatically released. At first, Brown's design failed to work as intended because the hooks securing the rafts disengaged too easily, but a solution was found by exchanging them for a more resilient design, manufactured by Mills Atlas and, thereafter, the davit and raft system performed reliably.

So far as the bow doors were concerned, the Royal Navy required a clam-shell design, hinged

cranes!' This equipment was all made at George Brown & Co.'s yard, the hatch covers being particularly thoroughly insulated to ensure that cargos of frozen fish would not be at risk of thawing. The vessel, named *Hofsjökull*, was delivered in 1964.

A prestigious contract was then gained from the Royal Navy to supply bow door operating systems and davits to launch inflatable life rafts for five new Royal Fleet Auxiliary landing craft – the 6,390gt *Sir Galahad* and *Sir Geraint*, to be built at Alexander Stephen & Sons shipyard at Linthouse on the Clyde, and *Sir Bedivere*, *Sir Tristram* and

BELOW: The MOD stores support vessel RFA *Tabartness* nears completion at Swan Hunter's Wallsend shipyard in 1967. The twelve Cargospeed doors were located in the recessed areas of hull topside ahead of the superstructure and forward and aft of the funnel. *(Jack Brown collection)*

ABOVE: British Rail's drive-through ferry **Antrim Princess**, delivered in 1967 by Hawthorn, Leslie Ltd of Hebburn-on-Tyne, catches morning sunlight while manoeuvring off her berth at Stranraer shortly after entering service on the route to Larne. (*Bruce Peter collection*)

LEFT: The **Antrim Princess**' bow visor in a half-open position, clearly showing the curving cut-line in her shell plating. (*Jack Brown collection*)

RIGHT: One of the hinged arms on the forward mooring deck by which the visor was attached to the hull. When in the closed position, cleats were engaged at regular intervals around the visor's perimeter to securely attach it to the hull, preventing upward wave pressure from forcing it open. (*Jack Brown collection*)

BELOW: Part of the folding platform deck system attached to the inside of the **Antrim Princess**' shell framing. (*Jack Brown collection*)

on either side of the bow opening. On the *Sir Lancelot*, MacGregor's doors had a very visible gap around the perimeter due to the hinge point being too close to the shell plating. Cargospeed's version located the hinges on arms so that the doors and shell plating on the subsequent five vessels was entirely flush – a simple solution that looked neater and also made maintenance easier by removing a crevice in which salt water could lodge, causing corrosion.

Cargospeed's contracts for the five RFAs were followed by three further naval orders to help equip the Ministry of Defence's three forthcoming stores support vessels, the 14,113gt *Lyness*, *Stromness* and *Tarbatness*, which were building at the Swan Hunter shipyard. Their purpose was to re-supply warships and RFA craft with ship's stores and munitions while at sea. A zip-wire transit system was used to send supplies to other naval vessels, sailing in parallel. Stores were brought up from the holds on elevators then were moved sideways and out through opened Cargospeed watertight doors at three positions on either beam. The doors were hung on KONEX hinges and made watertight by Seadog seals. The 12 doors on each vessel were opened and closed by miniature Hydromite power packs (supplied by Keelavite), mounted adjacent to each door to minimise hydraulic pipework.

In 1967, Cargospeed supplied a stern door for the 1,109gt freight ferry *Seaway Princess*, built by the Hong Kong & Whampoa Dockyard Co. for the Northern Steamship Company of Auckland's cargo service connecting New Zealand's North and South islands. Brown thought that as roll-on, roll-off port facilities in New Zealand were limited and the Union Steamship Company had priority to use the only ferry linkspan in Onehunga

(Auckland) and similarly in Lyttleton (Christchurch), it would be best to incorporate as much operational flexibility as possible into the *Seaway Princess*' design.

He speculatively designed a complex side-loading system to enable vehicles to drive on and off the vessel at wharves without any special shore infrastructure and at all states of the tide. This consisted of an elevating self-levelling platform inboard of the shell plating, connected to the main freight deck by a hinged ramp and with a folding ramp to reach the quay. Probably to avoid going over budget, the Northern Steamship Company's directorate decided against this solution and so the *Seaway Princess* was completed as a conventional stern loader. Brown subsequently learned that her service was indeed subjected to delays on account of having to wait for the Union Steamship Company's ferries to vacate the ro-ro berths – but he kept in mind the idea of using a self-levelling platform/ramp complex for subsequent projects.

British Rail's 3,730gt *Antrim Princess* for the Stranraer-Larne route was Cargospeed's first project to design and supply a bow door for a vessel intended for civilian service. It was on this notoriously exposed passage of the northern Irish Sea that the stern-loading *Princess Victoria* had foundered 15 years previously. In the period since, Townsend Ferries Ltd had successfully introduced the drive-through *Free Enterprise II* and *Free Enterprise III* on the Dover Strait, while British Rail's Caledonian Steam Packet Company subsidiary had since 1965 chartered the Swedish Stena Line ferry *Stena Nordica* for the Stranraer-Larne route, also with bow and stern doors (as she flew the Swedish flag, she was not subject to British regulations). In comparison with the route's

ABOVE: The Burns Laird Ardrossan-Belfast ferry *Lion* is seen in evening light at Ardrossan shortly after entering service in 1967. *(A. Ernest Glen)*

LEFT: Unfolding the initial section of one of the *Lion*'s platform decks with the other part still folded up against the shipside casing. *(Jack Brown collection)*

RIGHT: The second stage of the process involved arms, travelling on rails in the deck-head, being moved half way towards the centre-line so that the outer half of the platform deck could be folded down, filling the gap between the arms and the shell plating. What previously were platforms stowed next to the shell plating ended up being lowered adjacent to the centre-line. *(Jack Brown collection)*

ABOVE: The *Lion*'s vehicle deck, showing three out of four platform decks in operation with an inner platform folded upwards and the ends of the three in use hinged down for vehicle loading to occur. As can be seen on the left-hand-side, the hinging to make ramps was achieved by unhooking the travelling arms and paying out steel rope to lower the platforms to the main vehicle deck level. *(Jack Brown collection)*

ABOVE: The **Bencruachan** of 1968 was built by Charles Connell & Co. Ltd of Glasgow for Ben Line (William Thomson & Co. Ltd). The vessel featured Cargospeed Velle 'Shipshape' cranes and shell doors with folding pallet platforms. *(Jack Brown collection)*

principal existing vessel, the Wm Denny & Co-built *Caledonian Princess* of 1961, which was a stern-loader, the *Stena Nordica* had impressed on account of her speed of loading and discharge. So far as the British marine safety authorities were concerned, however, bow doors raised suspicion with regard to their possible lack of resilience in head-seas and so Townsend's two drive-through ferries had collision bulkheads with watertight inner ramps set well back from their bow visors.

As with the *Holyhead Ferry I*, the *Antrim Princess* was designed largely by British Rail's naval architects Tony Rogan and Don Ripley and built by Hawthorn Leslie & Co. Rogan and Ripley devised the vessel's hull form; this was relatively fine-lined at the bow and with a more vertical stem than was typical on recent Scandinavian ferries to lessen the upward force exerted by high waves hitting the visor. Her slender form slightly reduced the area of the vehicle deck – especially as the collision bulkhead and inner ramp were also set well back – but the design's enhanced safety margin was admirable. The task of defining the location and shape of the cut between the visor and the hull's topsides was given to Jack Brown's Cargospeed colleague, Ron Ballantyne. This required careful design work as, due to the hull's flare, the join and hence the watertight seal were three-dimensional, making it harder to achieve a tight connection all around the perimeter. To lock the visor, wedge cleats with opposite rotations were selected to give a

LEFT: Fabrication of Velle cranes at the Garvel Shipyard in the mid-1960s with sections of masts and top cross-trees taking shape; the recently installed overhead travelling cranes speeded up production. *(Jack Brown collection)*

TOP LEFT, CENTRE & RIGHT: A Cargospeed shell door, retrofitted on Blue Star Line's *Fremantle Star*. The left and centre images show the considerable stiffening added to the exterior of the vessel's shell plating around the hatch opening while the right-hand image shows the retractable pallet platform designed by Jack Brown unfolded outboard of the hull – a belated realisation of a version of the 'finger platform' concept he had devised almost a decade previously. *(Jack Brown collection)*

CENTRE LEFT: Cargospeed Velle 'Shipshape' cranes are shown in the process of fabrication in George Brown & Co (Marine) Ltd's Garvel shipyard in 1967 for Reardon Smith's bulk carrier *Welsh City*. Built upriver by Fairfield Shipbuilding and Engineering, the vessel was delivered in 1968. *(Jack Brown collection)*

CENTRE RIGHT: A pallet platform on the *Fremantle Star* extended; the platform folds inward through 180 degrees to lie flush on the 'tween deck. *(Jack Brown collection)*

RIGHT: Shown undergoing trials off Arran in the Firth of Clyde, Ben Line's splendid motor cargo liner *Benlawers* was built by Upper Clyde Shipbuilders (the former Charles Connell & Co.) and delivered in 1970. She was the final conventional general cargo vessel delivered new to the fleet and, shortly after, three West German-built container ships were commissioned. As with the earlier *Bencruachan*, she had a Cargospeed Velle 'Shipshape' crane, hatch covers and shell doors. *(Jack Brown collection)*

LEFT: Sections for a Velle crane mast are shown undergoing fabrication, then being welded together to form a complete unit. *(Jack Brown collection)*

RIGHT: An automatic boom welder, purchased by George Brown & Co. at the end of the 1960s superseded the need for a lot of manual welding. The welding head and actuating mechanism is mounted on a long boom, which could extend the length of the interior of a mast and could complete a weld from one end to the other. *(Jack Brown collection)*

balanced force. Subsequently, Cargospeed used these for numerous other ferry bow- and stern door installations. The *Antrim Princess'* platform decks were single lane panels, which hinged upwards on travelling sheaves (steel pulley wheels) to give more headroom for freight.

The 3,333gt *Lion*, another drive-through ferry with Cargospeed equipment for service across the northern Irish Sea, entered service very soon after the *Antrim Princess*. Her owner, Burns-Laird & Co., was a subsidiary of the Coast Lines Group which had run long-established passenger, cargo, mail and cattle-carrying services from Glasgow and Ardrossan to Belfast and elsewhere in Ireland. The new ferry would supersede what remained of this network, concentrating traffic on a single Ardrossan-Belfast link.

Built by Cammell Laird & Co. of Birkenhead, the *Lion* could carry as many as 250 cars, whereas the *Antrim Princess* accommodated only 155 in a hull with almost identical dimensions. The reason was that, while the latter had folding platform decks only one lane wide, the *Lion* had a much more sophisticated system, enabling the entire vehicle deck to carry two levels of cars during holiday peaks and freight on one level for the rest of the time.

Designing ferries requires a compromise between the finest hull lines for speed and fuel

LEFT: The strikingly modern and prestigious Cunard flagship **Queen Elizabeth 2**, photographed while on trials in 1969, featured a unique Cargospeed hatch cover system to maximise the capacity of her forward hold. *(Bruce Peter collection)*

TOP LEFT: Jack Brown (wearing bowler hat – at that time still the standard gear of a Clydeside shipyard manager) tests the controls for the *Queen Elizabeth 2*'s multiple sequentially-actuated hatch covers in her forward trunking. *(Jack Brown collection)*

TOP RIGHT: A view looking upwards through the *Queen Elizabeth 2*'s trunking, showing the folding hatch covers between each deck level in their open positions. *(Jack Brown collection)*

economy and the greatest internal volume for the biggest payload. To achieve an adequate stability margin, it is necessary to keep the centre of gravity as low as possible. On the *Lion*, it was decided that, rather than hoisting the platform decks up to the deckhead when not in use, it would be better to fold them parallel with the casings on either beam. That way, a couple of feet of free height could be saved and

consequently the top weight of the superstructure would be lower, with a positive effect on overall stability.

A further requirement was to enable either the whole upper vehicle deck area to be covered by mezzanine level platform decks, or half, or a quarter, depending on the mix of private cars or commercial vehicles to be carried on any given crossing. The solution was to fit tracks to the

BELOW: The *Queen Elizabeth 2*'s foredeck with the Cargospeed weather deck hatch covers folded open. *(Jack Brown collection)*

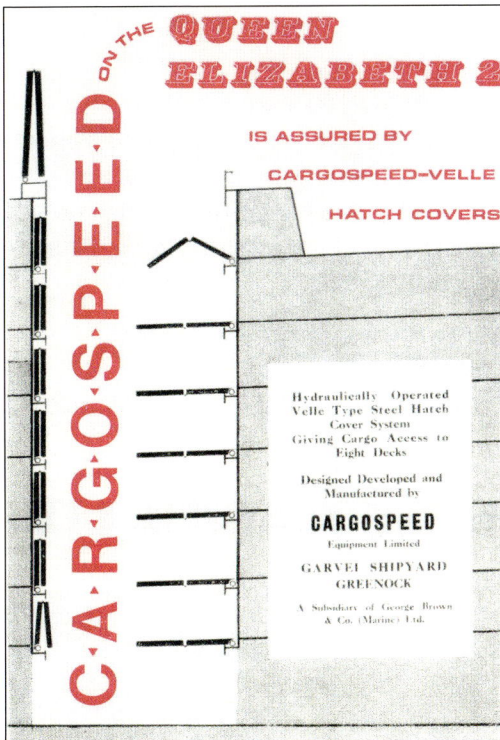

elegant but even though it worked reliably it remained unique to the *Lion*. Other ferry operators found that, on nearly all crossings, a mix of cars and commercial vehicles were carried and so investing a great deal extra in such sophisticated car deck equipment for the rare occasions when only cars or trucks were being carried was unnecessary.

The latter 1960s and early 1970s were a busy period for Cargospeed and consequently also for George Brown & Co. Apart from equipping several notable British ferries with vehicle access

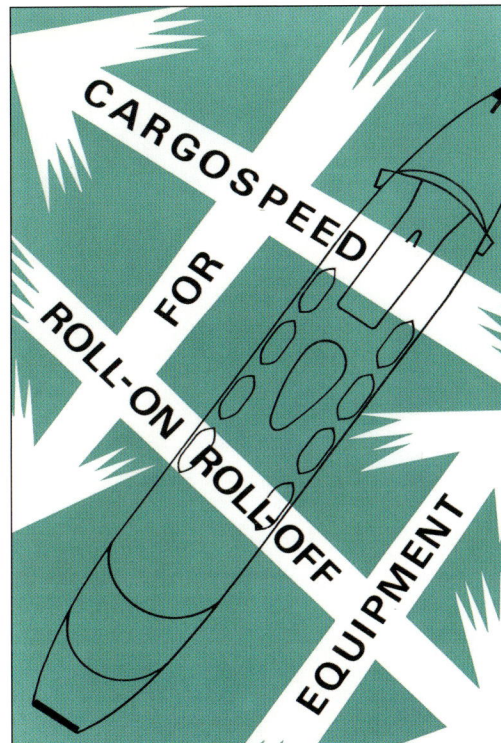

deckhead, in which suspension pillars could travel inboard from each side casing to a point half way between the casing and the centre line. The platform deck panels would be hinged from each side of the lower ends of the pillars, folding downwards like a butterfly's wings. Thanks to an ingenious system of hydraulics and steel wires, folding down the inboard platforms caused the suspension pillars to move away from the casings to the inner end of each track and back when the platforms were folded up. As with all the best mechanical engineering solutions, the design was

LEFT: Cargospeed's involvement in equipping the **Queen Elizabeth 2** was widely advertised in the latter 1960s and early 1970s. An advertisement from *The Glasgow Herald*'s special QE2 supplement shows how the liner's hatch covers were configured. *(Jack Brown collection)*

LEFT: The front page of a 1965 brochure, emphasising Cargospeed's commitment to the advancement of roll-on, roll-off vehicle access technologies. *(Jack Brown collection)*

LEFT: The launching of British Rail's multi-purpose Channel ferry **Vortigern**, completed in 1969 by Swan Hunter Shipbuilding Ltd of Newcastle. She was fitted with ingeniously designed Cargospeed bow and stern vehicle deck doors and elevating platform decks. *(Bruce Peter collection)*

doors and hoistable car deck equipment, the business of manufacturing Velle 'Shipshape' cranes and Velle hatch covers continued to be a lucrative earner. By the latter 1960s, some British liner companies – particularly Ben Line and Blue Star Line – belatedly sought to emulate their Scandinavian counterparts by using forklift trucks to shift consignments on palettes. Ben Line ran an express service, linking UK and Far East ports while Blue Star Line operated to North and South America and to Australia. In 1968-69, Cargospeed supplied shell doors for fitting at 'tween deck height towards the stern on the 12,011gt *Benstac* and the 12,892gt

Bencruachan, delivered in 1968 respectively by Charles Connell & Co. and its successor, Upper Clyde Shipbuilders. The shell doors opened outwards and to the side on substantial hinge arms, similar to those used for the bow doors on the five *Sir Galahad*-class vessels. Similar shell doors were retrofitted amidships on the 8,403gt *Freemantle Star* (a vessel originally built in 1960). Additionally, Velle cranes were manufactured for the *Benstac* and *Bencruachan*. Sadly, these fine ships had dismally short careers as, in the 1970s, the Europe-Far East route was containerised and so they were withdrawn and sold, in the case of the *Bencruachan* for scrapping after an existence

of no more than 12 years.

A very prestigious Cargospeed commission in the latter 1960s was to manufacture cargo hatch covers for the new Cunard flagship trans-Atlantic passenger liner known as Q4 until launched as the *Queen Elizabeth 2* – a vessel intended as a showcase for British shipbuilding expertise and the flagship of the UK merchant fleet. When the possibility of a novel installation occurred to Jack Brown, he contacted Cunard's Chief Naval Architect, Dan Wallace, who invited him to a meeting at the Line's grand Liverpool headquarters. Typically, on passenger liners, hatches for loading ship's stores, mail and general cargo were located towards the bow and sometimes also near the stern on the weather deck with a long vertical trunkway cutting through the passenger decks to the cargo hold at the bottom of the hull. Brown reasoned that the empty trunkway wasted a lot of space and so he got the idea of designing intermediate hatch covers, one at each deck level which could be closed sequentially as each deck was filled with cargo. Dan Wallace and his colleagues quickly saw the advantages of Brown's proposition, but worried that it would be necessary to use large quantities of intrusive hydraulic piping. Brown's solution was to use KONEX hydraulic hinges with adjacent Hydromite electric power packs to open and close each hatch – the same kind as had been installed to operate the doors on the MOD stores support ships *Lyness*, *Stromness* and *Tarbatness*. By carefully designing the electrical installation, it was possible to ensure that the *Queen Elizabeth 2*'s internal hatches would only work in sequence as the operator could only open a hatch cover he could see, or close the one immediately above it.

Following the *Queen Elizabeth 2* project, for the next few years, one of Cargospeed's most regular clients was British Rail, which commissioned a succession of new diesel-powered ro-ro ferries for its Irish and Continental ferry routes. In bidding to supply door, ramp and platform deck equipment for these vessels, Cargospeed competed with MacGregor – but thanks to Jack Brown's good relationship with BR's naval architects, Tony Rogan and Don Ripley, it was possible to gain a slight advantage by producing solutions closely tailored to their wishes. Whereas typical MacGregor offerings were supplied in pieces, leaving shipyards with the challenge of assembling them with sufficient precision to work reliably, Cargospeed's were delivered as complete pre-tested units, ready for installation. One such innovation of Brown's was a jigger-gear system, comprising a robust steel frame containing hydraulic cylinders with sheaves at the corners through which steel cables were threaded to actuate the movement of ferry platform decks. The jigger-units were supplied ready for welding in position in the deckhead of the vehicle deck. The design became popular with shipyards building ferries, giving Cargospeed a brief commercial advantage.

British Rail's 4,760gt *Vortigern* was a multi-purpose ship, designed to carry either trains, or 240 cars, or a mix of cars and commercial vehicles, and up to 1,000 passengers between

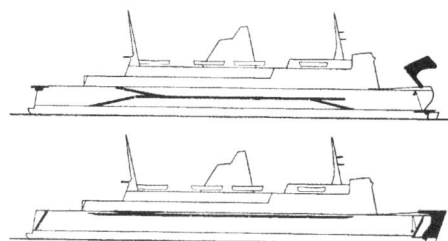

M.V. "VORTIGERN"
Versatility with cargospeed

- Elevating car decks and ramps
- Stern door
- Bow door/ramp
- Rising buffer beam
- Bow visor operating equipment
- Bow rudder locking pin
- Garage ramps

All hydraulically operated

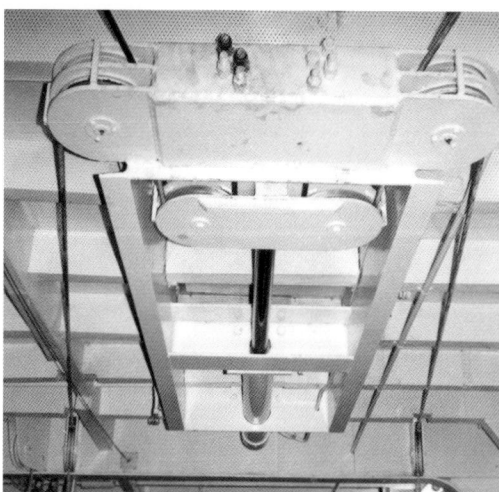

Dover and Boulogne in summer and from Dover
to Dunkerque in winter. Ordered from Swan
Hunter's Wallsend shipyard for delivery in 1969,
the *Vortigern* was technically – and in terms of
layout – a relatively complex ferry.

When carrying road vehicles, the *Vortigern* was
a drive-through vessel but, in train ferry mode, she
loaded via the stern only, meaning that a buffer

beam was needed at the forward end of her rail
tracks. If fixed to the deck, however, this would
block access to the bow door. Making a virtue out
of necessity, Brown used the lowering motion of
the bow access ramp to pull steel cables
threaded through sheaves in the deckhead and
attached to the buffer beam to lift it up. The
Vortigern's stern door was in two panels, the
upper of which was actuated by a KONEX hinge
with the lower panel connected to the upper by
hinges and guided by links to fold neatly
underneath.

As numbers of passengers and cars were
expected to fluctuate between the *Vortigern*'s two
routes, she was fitted with a hoistable mezzanine
vehicle deck system consisting of elevating
platforms (rather than the folding variety). Each
platform was raised and lowered from the
deckhead on steel ropes attached at each corner
and fed through sheaves to a jigger-unit. In
addition, the aft section of the *Vortigern*'s
superstructure on Main Deck had a convertible
space which could be used either as a passenger
deck saloon or as an additional upper garage for

LEFT: The *Vortigern*'s vehicle deck, showing the inner platform decks in their raised position with the outer platforms lowered. By raising all of the platforms to the deck-head, trains could be loaded on the ferry's four railway tracks. *(Bruce Peter collection)*

ABOVE: The British-owned, though French-flagged A.L.A. (Angleterre-Loraine-Alsace) Dover Strait passenger, road vehicle and train ferry **Saint Eloi** was a near-sister of the **Vortigern**. The Cargospeed stern door is visible in this picture. Ordered in 1972 from an Italian shipyard, Cantieri Navali di Pietra Ligure, her construction was beset by delays caused by the yard's perilous financial state and so she did not enter service until 1975. (Miles Cowsill)

cars. Docked stern-in at Dover, cars were loaded over the aft mooring deck but, berthed bow-first at Boulogne, they were unloaded via sections of platform deck that were raised at one end to Main Deck height. Thus, motorists whose vehicles were garaged in the convertible space needed to drive down first one ramp to Mezzanine Deck level and then down another to the main vehicle and train deck.

In Dover Strait service, the *Vortigern*'s flexible design proved a great success, so much so that it spawned two subsequent near-sisters, SNCF's

Chartres (1974) and ALA's *Saint Eloi* (1975).

Once the *Vortigern* project was underway, Cargospeed gained a smaller but welcome contract to manufacture the stern ramp for a new David MacBrayne ferry for the service from West Loch Tarbert to the island of Islay. Built by Ailsa Shipbuilding of Troon, the 1,324gt vessel entered service in 1970 as the *Iona*, not on the route for which she had been intended but instead on the Caledonian Steam Packet Company's Gourock-Dunoon crossing of the Firth of Clyde.

In Australia, Keith Holyman – whom Jack

RIGHT: The SNCF ferry **Chartres** was a further iteration of the **Vortigern**'s overall design. Built by the Dubigeon-Normandie shipyard at Nantes, she entered service in 1974 between Dover and Dunkerque and was fitted with Cargospeed bow and stern doors plus elevating platform decks. (Bruce Peter collection)

RIGHT: Three diagrams showing the positions achievable with the **Chartres**' stern door: left, the door is closed, centre it is open for berthing at long shore linkspans (as at Dover) and, right, it is open for berthing at short shore ramps. (Jack Brown collection)

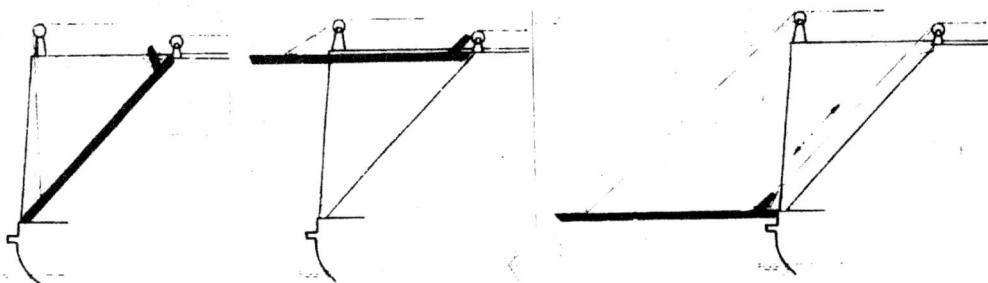

ABOVE: The David MacBrayne-owned car ferry **Iona** was built in 1970 by Alisa Shipbuilding of Troon. Intended for operation to the island of Islay, she actually entered service for the Caledonian Steam Packet Company between Gourock and Dunoon. Here, she is shown off Gourock Pier at an angle emphasising her Cargospeed stern ramp. *(Bruce Peter collection)*

Brown had visited in 1956 and failed to persuade to invest in roll-on, roll-off ferry tonnage – finally decided to make that leap. Realising that his company would not be allowed to use Australian National Line's berths in Australian and Tasmanian ports, he contacted Brown – with whom he had a good rapport – to design a stern-loading ro-ro freight ferry with cargo-handling gear capable of operating independently of ferry linkspans. Named the *Mary Holyman*, the 2,577gt vessel, built in the Netherlands by Boeles Scheeps & Machinfabriken of Bolnes, had an aft-located superstructure and three levels of garage space, consisting of a tank-top forward of the engine

LEFT: During the 1970s, Cargospeed exhibited their products and services at numerous international maritime industry exhibitions and conferences in the hope of attracting new orders. The stand features display material and scale models in an aesthetic typical of the era. *(Jack Brown collection)*

Tidebridge
and the
'697' series

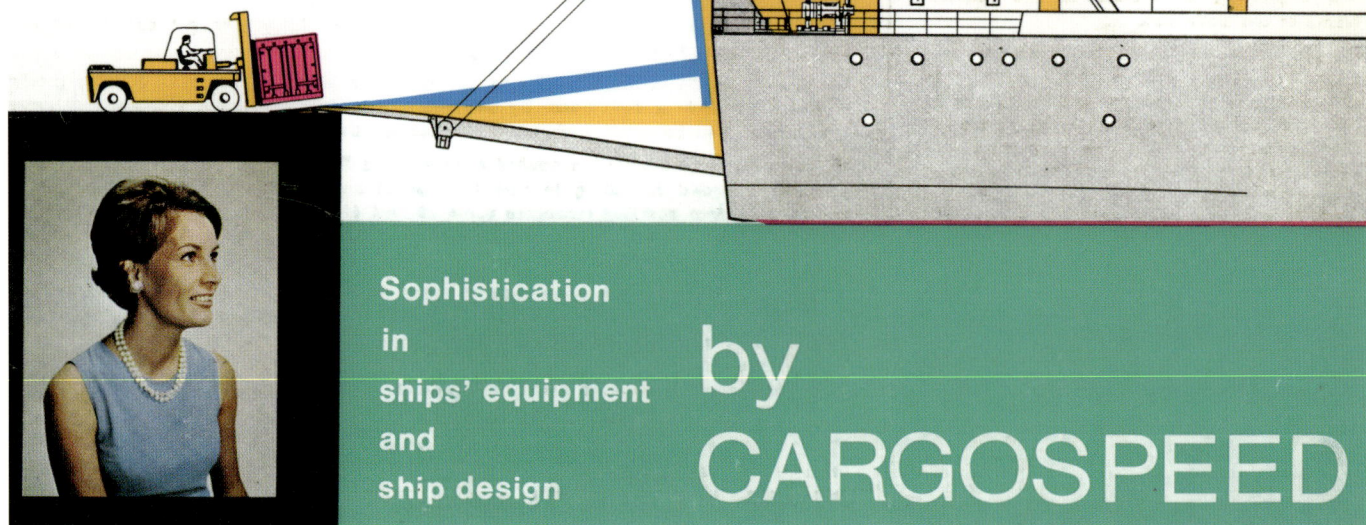

Sophistication
in
ships' equipment
and
ship design

by
CARGOSPEED

ABOVE: A Cargospeed brochure, promoting the 'Tidebridge' stern ramp system installed abroad the ro-ro freight vessel **Mary Holyman**, designed by Jack Brown; the drawing demonstrates how the system enabled the vessel to load and unload across a wide tidal and vessel draught range without any shore-based linkspan at ports on either side of the Bass Strait between Australia and Tasmania. (Jack Brown collection) (*Jack Brown collection*)

LEFT: The **Mary Holyman** is pictured off Greenock in 1971 when she made a single call to pick up a cargo of new containers while en-route from her builder Boele's Scheepswerven en Machinefabriek in the Netherlands to Tasmania, where she entered service across the Tasman Sea. (*Jack Brown collection*)

RIGHT: Loading containers in the James Watt dock, Greenock. (*Jack Brown collection*)

LEFT: **LEFT:** The view foreward from the ***Mary Holyman***'s stern, illustrating the fixed ramp to tank top level, which was accessed by hinging up a section of the main deck using a pair of hydraulic cylinders. Built in the form of an inverted girder bridge, this structure was supported safely in the open position by pairs of duplicated latches. (A more conventional solution on roll-on, roll-off vessels of the era was to enclose such a void in the deck with a series of side-opening hatch covers, adding both to weight and cost.) *(Jack Brown collection)*

BELOW: A profile drawing showing the fixed ramp, which began its descent in the space between the twin engines, with the main deck hinged up, showing the location of the hydraulic cylinders. *(Jack Brown collection)*

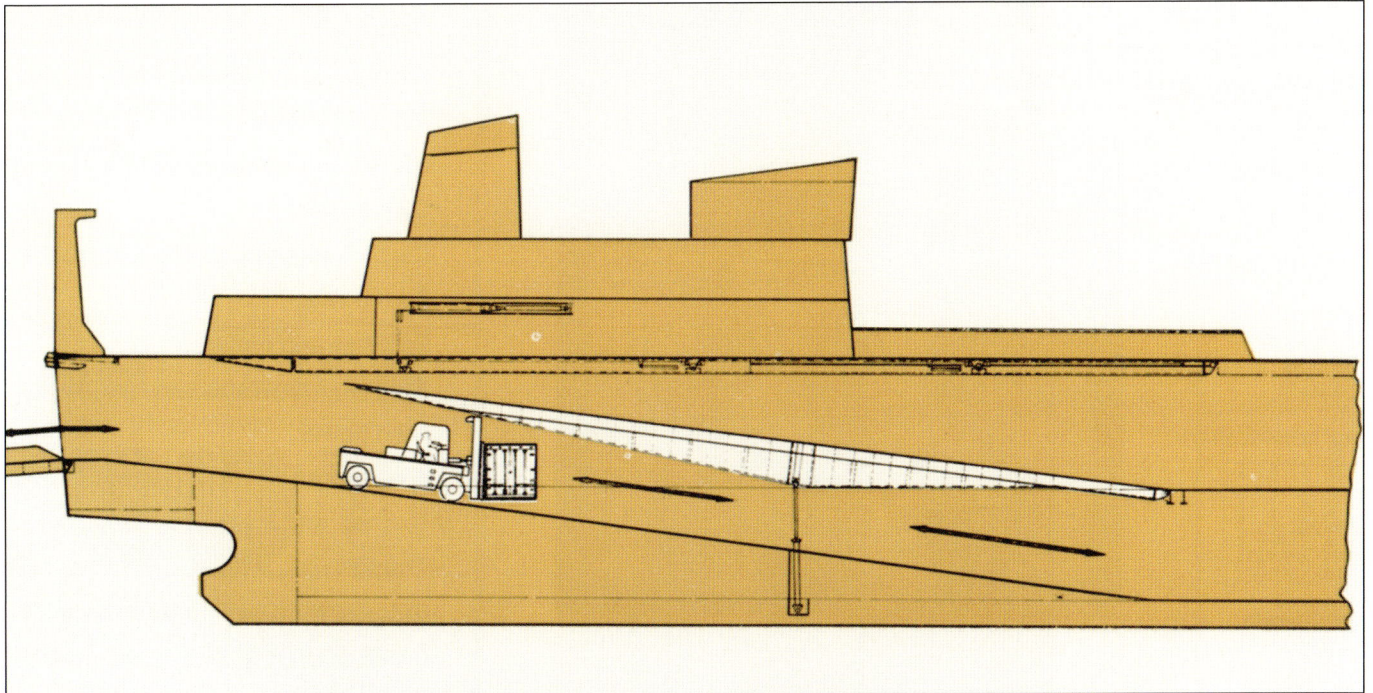

LEFT: The view up and aft from the ***Mary Holyman***'s tank-top level. *(Jack Brown collection)*

TOP: The view from the stern end of the **Mary Holyman**'s Main Deck, looking forward and showing the very long hoistable Weather Deck access ramp. *(Jack Brown collection)*

MIDDLE: A sectional drawing of the Weather Deck access ramp. *(Jack Brown collection)*

BOTTOM RIGHT: Inside the garage for new cars in the first tier of the superstruacure, showing the substantial jigger gear for operation of the Weather Deck ramp. This image shows the double rigging, which was in balanced tension to give a good safety margin. *(Jack Brown collection)*

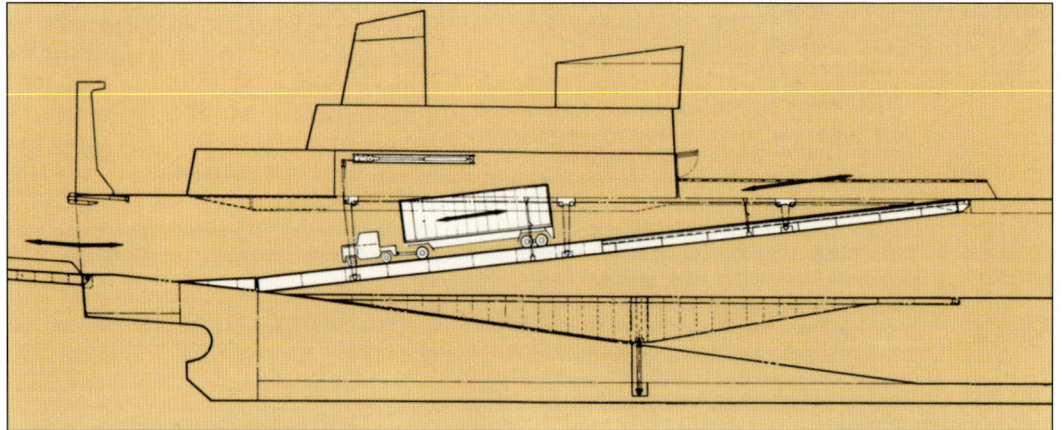

room, a fully enclosed main deck and an open weather deck.

Designing a stern-mounted ramp capable of use at extremes of the tidal range, coupled with ship trim and sinkage conditions, with a gradient of no more than 1 in 8 to allow trucks and trailers to be driven on and off, was a challenge. Brown commenced drawing the general arrangement plan by establishing an entry level in the transom which could meet the extremes within that up/down gradient. Working forward, and within the same 1 in 8 gradient, he drew in ramps from the main deck to the tank-top and to the weather deck, then developed the arrangement of the ship

around these ramps. The stern ramp would necessarily be long and therefore heavy, meaning that more robust operating gear than usual would be needed to open, close and support it during cargo operations. Its main section was akin to a girder bridge and actuated by a powerful winch, double-rigged in balanced tension for a high safety factor. Inboard, the *Mary Holyman* had a fixed ramp accessing the tank-top, enclosed at main deck level by an innovative ramp cover, which alone weighed 113 tons and was raised by two hydraulic cylinders. The 47-metre-long ramp from main to weather deck level was likewise double-rigged in balanced tension so that it could

be raised with trailers parked upon it once weather deck loading was complete. After her lengthy delivery voyage, the *Mary Holyman* went on to have a successful career traversing the Tasman Sea, lasting until 1988 when she was sold for further use in Mediterranean waters.

In 1971, Jack Brown established an additional company, Seaform Design, to promote designs for ferry ramp systems, supporting Cargospeed's business. That year, a new British Rail ferry for the Stranraer-Larne route was delivered from an Italian shipyard, Cantiere Navale Breda S.p.A., located near Venice. The 3,908gt *Ailsa Princess* was a near-sister of the *Antrim Princess*,

RIGHT: A forklift loads a container aboard the **Mary Holyman**; even although the tide appears to be low (as the discolouration of the quay wall would indicate), a combination of lless than load draught and the ramp's significant length enabled a gentle gradient to be maintained. *(Jack Brown collection)*

BELOW: A Cargospeed conversion table showing equivalent gradients; the **Mary Holyman**'s ramps were around 1 in 8. *(Jack Brown collection)*

EQUIVALENT GRADIENTS

Incline		Degrees		Percent
1 : 12	=	4.76°	=	8.3%
1 : 11	=	5.20°	=	9.1%
1 : 10	=	5.71°	=	10.0%
1 : 9	=	6.33°	=	11.1%
1 : 8	=	7.13°	=	12.5%
1 : 7	=	8.13°	=	14.3%
1 : 6	=	9.47°	=	16.7%
1 : 5	=	11.31°	=	20.0%
1 : 4	=	14.03°	=	25.0%

CARGOSPEED

FOR RO-RO ACCESS EQUIPMENT

described earlier, and the ro-ro access equipment supplied by Cargospeed was therefore similar, apart from a more extensive hoistable platform deck system. More innovative in that regard were three new ferries for Channel routes – the 5,596gt *Hengist* and *Horsa* and the 5,131gt *Senlac*. These were built to an exceptionally high quality by the Arsenal de la Marine National Francaise at Brest, which was a naval shipyard, and delivered between 1972 and 1973. The first two in the series were for Folkestone-Boulogne service while the last was to operate between Newhaven and Dieppe.

For these vessels, Jack Brown had the idea of fitting jigger units into the underside of each platform deck panel, reversing the usual solution of installing them in the deck head. Each panel had steel ropes threaded through sheaves at both ends which were attached to the jigger unit, and also threaded through sheaves in the deck head. By paying out or winding in rope at both ends of each panel, it could be lowered or raised to the deck head. When a panel was lowered to mezzanine height, continuing to pay out rope from one end would lower it down to the main vehicle deck, converting it into an access ramp for the

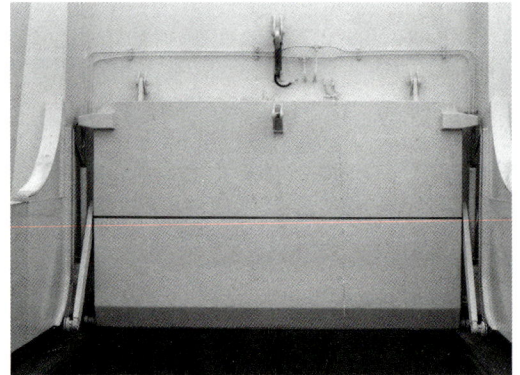

LEFT: An exterior view from weather deck level, showing the view aft down the ramp towards the superstructure, where a watertight door enclosed the car garage space above when the vessel put to sea. *(Jack Brown collection)*

TOP RIGHT: The car garage access watertight door in the closed position. *Jack Brown collection)*

BOTTOM RIGHT: The car garage access door open with the ramp raised to Weather Deck level to enable cars to be parked in the garage. *Jack Brown collection)*

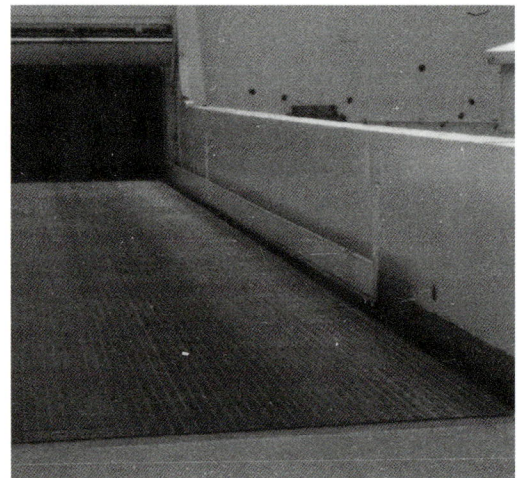

LEFT & BELOW: A model of a design by Jack Brown for a version of the Tidebridge concept, known as a 'Curved Tidebridge'; this retained all of the benefits of an axial Tidebridge with the advantage of operating to a normal quayside berth. The design would have been mounted in a recess in a conventional transom stern on a ship's centre line and would also have been a shorter, lighter and simpler structure than a standard stern-quarter ramp. This would have avoided the need to cut off the corner of the stern and therefore avoided an undesirable 'heeling moment'. *(Jack Brown collection)*

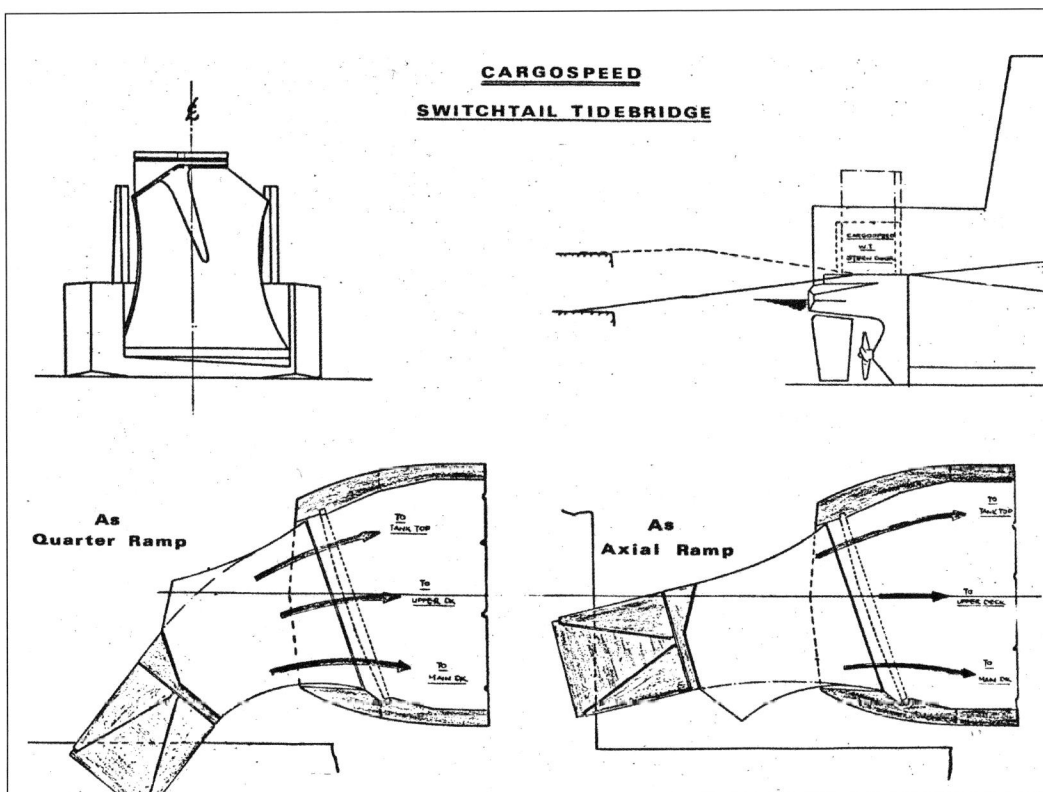

CARGOSPEED
SWITCHTAIL TIDEBRIDGE

As
Quarter Ramp

As
Axial Ramp

LEFT: Diagrams of a 'switchtail' version of a curved Tidebridge, capable of operating either as a quarter-ramp, or an axial ramp; the outer triangulated ramp panels can be switched from one position to the other. *(Jack Brown collection)*

ABOVE: British Rail's **Ailsa Princess** of 1971 was built by Cantiere Navale Breda in Italy as a partner for the **Antrim Princess** on the Stranraer-Larne route. She was fitted with Cargospeed bow and stern vehicle deck doors and elevating platform decks (as opposed to the folding variant installed on her elder sister). *(Bruce Peter collection)*

remainder of the platform deck.

The *Hengist*, *Horsa* and *Senlac* had two longitudinal casings, each approximately a third of the way across the width of the vehicle deck and there were hoistable platform decks consisting of panels of the type described previously in all three sections. This enabled a very high degree of flexibility in comparison with the majority of ferries at that time, on which the platform decks only had ramps at each end, meaning that either the whole platform length could be used or none at all. As

every platform section on the new ferries could double as a ramp, the mix of double- and single-deck-high space could be varied, depending on the mix of cars and commercial vehicles to be carried on any given crossing.

The problem of supplying hydraulic fluid to the jigger units was resolved by using carefully positioned loops of flexible tubing. As with previous Cargospeed design innovations, the solution arrived at for the *Hengist*, *Horsa* and *Senlac* was as ingenious as it was elegant in its

RIGHT: The highly successful Cargospeed-equipped British Rail Channel ferry **Hengist** is shown while under construction at the Arsenal de la Marine National Francaise at Brest in France during the winter of 1971-72. *(Bruce Peter collection)*

simplicity.

In early 1971 Jack Brown received a surprise telex message from Jim Murray, a director of Federal Commerce & Navigation Ltd in Montreal, including an invitation to visit the Copenhagen offices of the naval architects Knud E. Hansen A/S for briefing. Part of the surprise was that 14 years previously, Murray had been a classmate of Brown's at Glasgow Academy.

Murray and naval architects from Knud E. Hansen A/S wanted to discuss with Brown the possibility of Cargospeed designing and supplying extensive ro-ro equipment for two unusually complicated paper and car carriers, the 16,284gt *Laurentian Forest* and *Avon Forest*. These were being designed for trans-Atlantic service between ports on the St Lawrence River in Canada and Avonmouth in the UK. The primary reason for their complexity was the need to carry an entirely different cargo in each direction. Westbound, large rolls of paper would be shipped on pallets on three internal decks, whereas Eastbound British-made cars would be carried on seven decks, meaning between the three paper decks, four mezzanine decks would be lowered. As the entire mezzanine deck, ramp and lift installation would need to be relatively light in weight so as not to reduce the vessels' deadweight capacity, the use of conventional ferry-type steel platforms, raised and lowered by hydraulic equipment, would be out of the question. In addition, the vessels would need to operate independently of

specialist shore-based infrastructure and so large ship-to-shore ramps that could be adjusted to offset tide, trim and sinkage would be essential.

Brown found out that heavy-duty straddle-carriers would be used to load the paper rolls, stacked on large pallets. On board, the straddle-carriers would drop the pallets on cargo elevators serving the lower decks, from where the individual rolls would be picked up by forklift clamp trucks for stowage. Once cleared, the empty pallets would be returned to the main deck level from where the straddle-carriers would take them ashore.

Attending the discussions in Copenhagen was Duncan Maxwell a director of Port Weller Dry Dock Ltd, the Canadian yard tendering for the vessels. It emerged from the discussions that

BELOW: A general view of the *Hengist*'s vehicle deck, showing the arrangement of the twin casings with three sets of elevating platform decks filling the spaces between. *(Jack Brown collection)*

TOP: The **Senlac** of 1973 was the last to be delivered of the class of three highly successful French-built, British Rail-owned Channel ferries fitted with Cargospeed equipment; she operated between Newhaven and Dieppe in consort with a pair of French-owned vessels. *(Bruce Peter collection)*

PWDD had negotiated an offer from the Canadian Government of a financial subsidy, but the grant would only be available for a contract placed by a cut-off date just a couple of weeks hence. Following several days of joint discussions in Copenhagen, Maxwell spent most of the following week in Greenock where Brown described in detail the multiple Cargospeed ro-ro items and the installation procedures involving PWDD. A contract for the two vessels was placed with PWDD, from whom Cargospeed – along with other suppliers – received an enquiry about the possibility of designing in detail and supplying all of the ro-ro equipment.

To bring paper rolls on board, Brown revived the three-part ramp complex system originally proposed for the *Seaway Princess*. Two of these would be fitted to each vessel, one forward on the starboard side of the hull and the other aft on the same side. The ramp complexes consisted of an athwartships ship-to-shore ramp which was joined to a self-levelling platform, from which a long fore-and-aft ramp connected to the main deck. This platform, which was raised and lowered by an ingenious hydraulic drive system, automatically adjusted to maintain the shore and ship ramps at the same gradients over the entire eight-metre tide and sinkage range.

Rather than leaving the ramps exposed, breaking the line of the shell plating at the bow and stern, it had been decided to equip the vessels with shell doors to give added protection from high Atlantic waves. These were envisaged by Knud E. Hansen A/S staff as side-hinging, but Brown proposed instead upward lifting doors, the exteriors shaped to continue the vessels' hull form

without interruption so as not to catch the waves. Each weighed 30 tons and was locked shut securely by roller cleats engaging with wedges all around the perimeter using a system Brown had previously devised and patented called 'Autocleat'. Operation was from large jigger gears, each of which was double-rigged in balanced tension. The perimeters of the door apertures contained heater elements behind neoprene twin chamber watertight seals to ensure that they would remain operational in Canadian winter ice conditions. As Lloyd's of London's naval architect Bob Lockhart was concerned that the large forward door opening in the hull would reduce the vessels' longitudinal strength, a substantial steel reinforcement beam was fabricated over the forecastle deck above to compensate for the door aperture. Although the doors were heavy and contained many novel features, in practice, they worked reliably. In appearance, the *Laurentian Forest* and *Avon Forest* more resembled medium-sized container ships than ro-ro vessels due to their lack of visible ramps.

The cargo elevators to carry the pallets of paper rolls from deck to deck were lowered and raised by Hagglunds hydraulic motors in deckhouses on the weather deck. From the corners of each elevator platform, four vertical steel ropes passed through sheaves located under the weather deckhead from where they were threaded diagonally to four separate deep grooves in a vertically mounted winch barrel. This inventive configuration of Brown's was simple but proved reliable and effective in operation.

Designing the four hoistable car deck levels – totalling almost 10,000 square metres – was a

ABOVE: A stern-quarter view of the remarkable paper and car carrier *Laurentian Forest*, the first of two sisters built in 1972 and 1973 by Port Weller Dry Docks Ltd in Canada and featuring extensive Cargospeed-supplied access equipment. *(Jack Brown collection)*

BELOW LEFT: Cargospeed 'Autocleat' after shell door in fully opened position. The 'Autocleat' rollers travelled in trackways, and in the closed position all rollers engaged simultaneously with wedges to secure the 31 tonne door watertight. *(Jack Brown collection)*

BELOW RIGHT: With the shell door fully opened, the vessel's ramp complex could operate over an eight metre tide and sinkage range. *(Jack Brown collection)*

The equipment on board for operation as a paper carrier

TOP LEFT: The *Laurentian Forest*'s forward shell door in the starboard bow quarter, showing the trackway for the 'Autocleat' rollers in the door frame. *(Jack Brown collection)*

CENTRE LEFT: The shore ramp of the Cargospeed 'Tidebrige' ramp complex. *(Jack Brown collection)*

BOTTOM LEFT: The self-levelling platform to which the shore ramp and the ship's internal ramp were attached; this adjusted automatically to keep both ramps at the same gradient. *(Jack Brown collection)*

TOP RIGHT: One of four elevators, the operating systems of which comprised of a vertical axis winch drum, feeding four ropes directly to large diameter sheaves and down to the corners of the winch platform. *(Jack Brown collection)*

UPPER CENTRE RIGHT: The winch drum with four deep grooves, feeding out or winding in four steel wire ropes simultaneously. *(Jack Brown collection)*

LOWER CENTRE RIGHT: One of the elevator openings at Main Deck level. *(Jack Brown collection)*

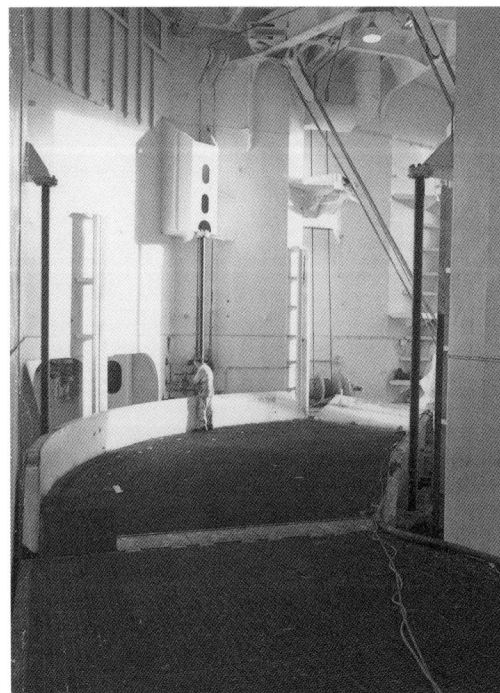

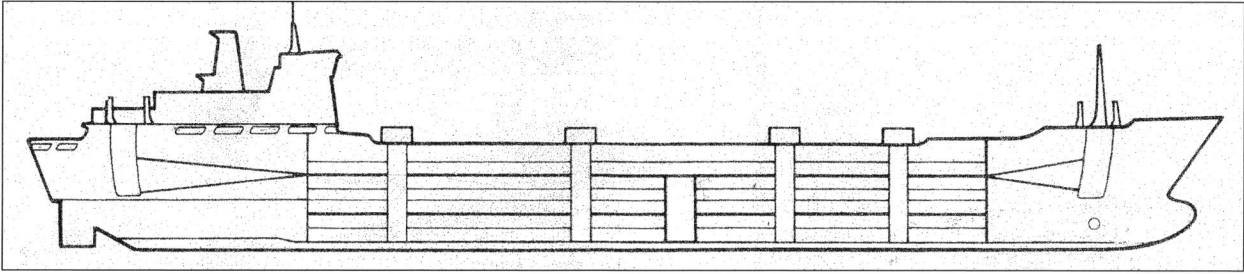

Eastbound from Canada to Britain

LEFT: A sectional profile drawing of the *Laurentian Forest*, showing the decks configured for the loading of paper rolls on the Tank-Top, Main Deck and Weather Deck for the eastbound voyage from Canada to Europe. *(Jack Brown collection)*

TOP LEFT: On arrival at Avonmouth, an empty straddle-carrier goes aboard the Laurentian Forest to collect paper rolls. *(Jack Brown collection)*

MIDDLE: A pallet being loaded with paper rolls at tank-top level. *(Jack Brown collection)*

BOTTOM LEFT: A loaded pallet approaching Main Deck level. *(Jack Brown collection)*

MIDDLE RIGHT: An arrival at Avonmouth, an empty straddle-carrier goes aboard the Laurentian Forest to collect paper rolls. *(Jack Brown collection)*

BOTTOM RIGHT: The loaded pallet is brought ashore by a straddle-carrier. *(Jack Brown collection)*

The equipment on board for operation as a car carrier

TOP LEFT: An 'Autocleat' sliding bulkhead door, spanning between the fixed decks, in the open position with lowered car platform decks on either side. *(Jack Brown collection)*

LEFT: The upper platform deck, accessed via two ramps from Main Deck below. *(Jack Brown collection)*

MIDDLE LEFT: To allow car ramps to be stowed in the deck head, where there was a deep transverse beam, these were constructed in three sections, which were lowered individually and connected together by short hinged panels. *(Jack Brown collection)*

BOTTOM LEFT: Almost uniquely, the car ramps also penetrated the watertight bulkheads, which had 'Autocleat' doors above and below to enable full bulkhead watertight closure, but the ramps to be lowered in port. *(Jack Brown collection)*

TOP RIGHT: A Mark 2 export Ford Cortina, passing through one of the watertight bulkheads; when the ramp was stowed, panels within the bulkheads lowered from above and raised from below to create a watertight seal. *(Jack Brown collection)*

RIGHT: One of the mobile scissors lifts – known as 'Fidos' used by deck crew to raise and lower the platform decks on the Laurentian Forest and her sister. *(Jack Brown collection)*

LOWER RIGHT: A view at 'tween deck level with two levels of car decks stowed in the deck head. *(Jack Brown collection)*

BOTTOM RIGHT: Main Deck with the platform decks lowered and car access ramps in the middle-distance. *(Jack Brown collection)*

TOP LEFT: A view from the upper of two platform decks below Main Deck, looking down a ramp feeding to lower levels. *(Jack Brown collection)*

LEFT: By the use of explosive nailing, much time and expense was saved in the construction of the hoistable car decks. The nails attached the structural plywood deck surfaces to the panel frameworks. *(Jack Brown collection)*

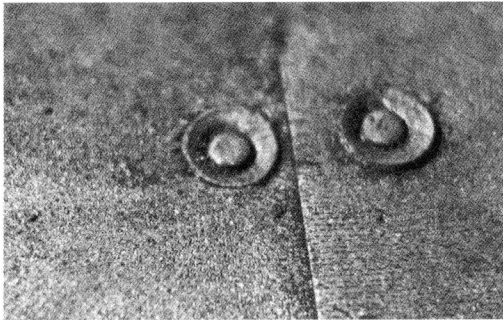

Westbound from Britain to Canada

MIDDLE LEFT: A Ford Cortina is driven though the Laurentian Forest's aft shell door. *(Jack Brown collection)*

BOTTOM LEFT: A Cortina transferring between two levels of platform deck. *(Jack Brown collection)*

TOP RIGHT: A van on the aft self-levelling platform. *(Jack Brown collection)*

MIDDLE RIGHT: MG coupés, tightly stowed on deck. *(Jack Brown collection)*

BOTTOM RIGHT: Some of the 2,200 cars awaiting loading at Avonmouth. *(Jack Brown collection)*

The twin vessels **Aberthaw Fisher** and **Kingsnorth Fisher** built in 1966 were the first vessels of their kind worldwide especially for the transport of very large (up to 300 tonnes) items for power generating stations. To secure watertight the top of the elevator shaft on each vessel, Cargospeed designed a unique horizontal stowing hatch cover.

TOP LEFT: View looking aft from the Aberthaw Fisher superstructure. Deck visible in the foreground; top of the hatch cover with suspension rollers in the middle, and top of the loading ramp towards the stern. *(Jack Brown collection)*

UPPER LEFT: View looking forward towards the superstructure from the top of the loading ramp. *(Jack Brown collection)*

MIDDLE LEFT: The top of the hatch cover showing the suspension rollers and quick-acting cleats. *(Jack Brown collection)*

TOP RIGHT: A Mark 2 export Ford Cortina, passing through one of the watertight bulkheads; when the ramp was stowed, panels within the bulkheads lowered from above and raised from below to create a watertight seal. *(Jack Brown collection)*

UPPER & MIDDLE RIGHT: A 330 tonnes test load rolling aboard to location on the hatch cover. *(Jack Brown collection)*

LOWER: The elevator shaft opened by rolling the hatch cover aft on lower rollers then transferring to the upper suspension rollers engaging in suspension trackways on the underside of the loading ramp. *(Jack Brown collection)*

The procedure showing how the hatch cover was transferred to suspended location on the underside of the loading ramp to give clear access for the elevator platform to level with the loading ramp. When the second of two 300 tonne loads had been lowered into the hold on the elevator platform, the hatch cover was returned to seal the elevator shaft. The closing procedure was the reverse of the opening procedure, and once the hatch cover was secured watertight a third 300 tonne load was positioned on the hatch cover for the voyage.

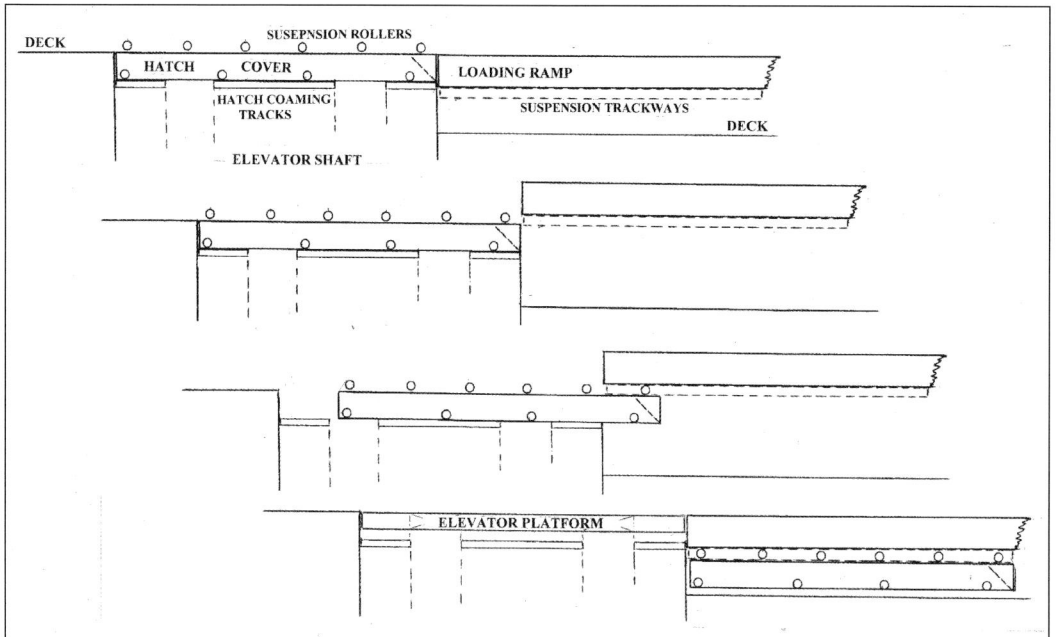

major project in itself. To save weight, Brown decided that it would be best to make each deck panel as a steel frame covered with panels of very strong industrial plywood made in Finland. To simplify the attachment of the plywood panels, an ingenious explosive nailing system was used to fire nails through both the plywood and the steel framework. To save additional weight and a great deal of expense, instead of fitting jigger units to each panel for hydraulic raising and lowering, mobile scissors lifts would be moved on the steel decks to beneath each panel needing moving. Once the *Laurentian Forest* and *Avon Forest* entered service, their deck crews referred to these mobile lifts as 'Fidos' because they had no driver's cabs and were instead controlled by a hand-held console on a lead. Moving them around the decks was therefore a bit like taking a dog for a walk.

The ramps giving car access to the composite steel/plywood car decks at lower levels could only be fitted in if they penetrated through transverse watertight bulkheads. A neat design solution was achieved whereby each ramp, in conjunction with two small vertically moving watertight door panels, combined to fill the hole in the bulkhead and in the deck opening above when in the stowed position. It is Brown's belief that these were the only watertight bulkhead-penetrating ramps anywhere in the world.

Cargospeed's contract with Port Weller Dry Dock Ltd to design in detail, manufacture and deliver all of the equipment described previously for the *Laurentian Forest* and *Avon Forest* was worth £2.5 million in total, making it the biggest in the company's history. Brown envisaged manufacturing all of the components in Greenock and so the costings were worked out accordingly. Unbeknown to him, in order to benefit from the Canadian Government subsidy for export orders, the vessels' operator, Federal Commerce & Navigation Ltd, had bought an existing British business, the Burnett Steamship Company, to be their legal owner. The Canadian Government consequently informed all the parties involved that, if the subsidy were to be paid, it would only be on the basis of all the cargo-handling equipment being manufactured in Canada, not in the UK.

Brown believed that this ultimatum would be impossible due to the equipment's specialist characteristics and so the management at Port Weller Dry Dock Ltd sent him to the Government in Ottawa to argue the case for manufacturing in Greenock. The outcome was a compromise whereby the car decks would be made in Canada, and everything else in Greenock. The night when Brown was in Ottawa preparing to fly home the next day, it was announced on the news that the Bretton Woods Gold Standard Agreement, ensuring a fixed pound-to-dollar

exchange rate, had been abandoned. Negotiated in 1944, the Bretton Woods system had ensured fixed rates of currency exchange by tying value levels to gold and preventing competitive devaluation. In August 1971 the USA ceased to ensure the dollar's parity with gold, thereby causing the Bretton Woods system to collapse. Brown tried desperately to contact Greenock to tell management there that he had the contracts and that a forward Canadian dollar/pound currency deal lined up with Williams & Glynn's bank in London should be activated immediately – but when he finally managed to get through, it was too late. The pound, US dollar and other currencies became free-floating. The reasons were that Vietnam War debt had led the dollar to be over-valued while spending on military and social programmes had made matters worse. In response, President Nixon issued an Executive Order ending controls over the level at which the dollar was valued relative to gold.

The consequence was that foreign exchanges closed down for a week, during which time the pound slipped in value against the Canadian dollar. As a result of this, Cargospeed's expected profit margin was wiped out. The equipment was supplied according to the agreed contract specifications, but Port Weller Dry Dock raised a host of invoices against Cargospeed for its involvements in installations which they claimed were insufficiently defined in Cargospeed's specifications. Brown, in a face-to-face meeting with PWDD directors, achieved some reductions and an understanding that it would take time to settle the remaining invoices. These were paid back over the ensuing three years, removing most of the profits from subsequent contracts.

From a technical point of view, the *Laurentian Forest* and *Avon Forest*'s unusual ro-ro cargo access equipment worked well and the vessels received extensive coverage in the professional journals. For Brown personally, they were the most challenging yet satisfying engineering projects of his career – but for Cargospeed and George Brown & Co. they proved a great economic disappointment. Both vessels were eventually sold to join the fleet of the American Military Sealift Command.

Worse was to follow. In 1973 the international shipping industry suffered a major blow when Arab nations in the Organisation of Petroleum Exporting Countries (OPEC) decided to retaliate against America and its allies to punish them for supporting Israel in the Yom Kippur War. By slashing oil production by between 5 and 10 per cent per month, they hoped to pressurise the West into forcing Israel to withdraw from the areas it had occupied. Since the Second World War, oil prices had remained more or less stable at around ten dollars a barrel but during the latter part of 1973 they quadrupled, precipitating a global downturn. In Britain, the repercussions of the Oil Crisis were felt throughout the economy and a cycle of inflation and currency instability began, making profiting from domestic and export orders all the harder.

Cargospeed had a healthy order book; the major problem was actually to earn a decent return on the contracts it had obtained. In 1974-75, three new British domestic ferries – Caledonian MacBrayne's 849gt *Jupiter* and *Juno* for the cross-Clyde Gourock-Dunoon service and P&O's 2,571gt *St Ola* for the stormy Pentland Firth crossing from Scrabster to Stromness on Orkney – received Cargospeed ro-ro access and vehicle deck equipment. The *Jupiter* and *Juno* were built by James Lamont & Co. in Greenock, a yard located near George Brown & Co.'s facility where the vessels' side and stern ramps were manufactured.

From the *Iona* onwards, it was standard Cargospeed practice on stern ramps to fit links between the ends of the rods of the operating cylinders and the connecting brackets on the ramps. These were given the name 'lazy links' and allowed the ramp to hinge up or down to contend with vessel trim changes and wave induced movements. While these worked admirably for the stern ramps which stowed less than vertical and lowered with the links in tension, the vertical stowage of the side ramps for the *Jupiter* and *Juno* would cause the links to flop and the ramps to 'clang' into their stowed positions. Brown came up with a novel solution which combined cushioning the closure with simultaneous engagement of the latches to secure the ramps while in passage; this combined a push-out of the ramp with unlatching upon lowering.

The *St Ola* was constructed by Hall, Russell & Co. in Aberdeen. The Cargospeed documentation supplied to the builder showing the bow visor operating arrangement included reference to the need to strengthen the hull structure sufficiently at the locations where the heels of the hydraulic cylinders opening the bow visor would exert maximum pressure on the surrounding structure. This reference was overlooked and unfortunately, when the visor was tested for the first time, it failed to move and instead the structure aft of the cylinder heels collapsed with a loud crunch. The yard quickly rebuilt and adequately reinforced the hull around the crucial pressure points.

In Canada, meanwhile, a contract was gained to supply bow and stern access doors for the 6,991gt Great Lakes ferry *Chi-Cheemaun*. She was built by Collingwood Shipyards in Ontario and delivered in 1974 to the Ministry of Highways for the Province of Ontario for its Lake Superior route from Tobermory to South Baymouth on Manitoulin Island. The bow visor, fabricated by the Collingwood yard, was the largest and heaviest in

Cargospeed's experience; this was due to the slender bow lines necessitating a cut in the hull far further aft than was usual on a ferry of the *Chi-Cheemaun*'s size and type.

In 1975, bow and stern vehicle deck doors were made for a new B&I (British and Irish) freight ferry, the 3,087gt *Dundalk*, built by the Verolme Cork Dockyard for operation between Liverpool, Holyhead and Dublin. As with the *Jupiter*, *Juno*, *St Ola* and the *Chi-Cheemaun* projects, the equipment for the *Dundalk* was based upon well-tested Cargospeed design precedents.

Far less conventional solutions were required when Cargospeed gained contracts to supply ro-ro equipment for a number of prominent Channel ferries for Townsend Thoresen. During the mid-1970s, it underwent a major expansion, masterminded by its go-ahead managing director, Keith Wickenden. Four new ferries were built at Aalborg Værft in 1975-76 for the Portsmouth-Cherbourg and Felixstowe-Zeebrugge routes. These were the 6,387gt *Viking Venturer*, *Viking Valiant*, *Viking Voyager* and *Viking Viscount*. Known as 'Super-Vikings', they were designed by Townsend Thoresen's in-house naval architect, James Ayers, with the assistance of his son, Michael. A great deal of redundancy and flexibility was demanded as Townsend Thoresen ferries experienced intensive usage.

For Jack Brown, a significant design challenge was to design a bow and stern door arrangement enabling the ferries to use not only the port facilities on their intended routes but also the ones at Dover in case they were ever needed to deputise on Townsend Thoresen's services from there to Zeebrugge, Calais or Boulogne. The problem was that the Portsmouth, Cherbourg, Felixstowe and Zeebrugge ferry berths were of a type requiring the vessels to provide the land bridge by lowering their long bow and stern ramps. At Dover and Calais, by contrast, there were linkspans aligning with forward and aft hull belting and so long folding ramps would get in the way. To enable Townsend Thoresen the flexibility it wanted, Brown designed special bow and stern ramps, each in two sections locked together by four hydraulically actuated shear pins. Inside the bow visor, there was a latch which could be connected to the upper section of the ramp. Thus, by actuating this arrangement, the ramp's topmost three-quarters could be attached to the inside of the bow visor after which the shear pins holding the two ramp sections together could be disconnected. This allowed it to be lifted away from the bow opening when the visor was raised. The remaining stump of ramp was lowered to a rectangular platform, fitting the berth at Calais. The stern door could either hinge down in one long piece at Portsmouth or Felixstowe, or its upper part could similarly be disengaged and hinged upwards to the deckhead.

The Blue Funnel Line cargo liner **Mentor** is seen in dry dock at Greenock in 1980. She is equipped with an impressive array of Cargospeed Velle 'Shipshape' cranes rigged on 'goalpost' masts. The installation was costly, but enabled the vessel to trade to ports without shore-based container handling cranes. *(Jack Brown collection)*

LEFT: The Blue Funnel Line cargo liner **Menelaus** is seen nearing completion in dry dock at Mitsubishi Heavy Industries in Nagasaki in 1977. She has a comprehensive installation of Cargospeed Velle 'Shipshape' cranes. The 'high-rise' masthouses and winch platforms enabled substantial container stowage on the hatch covers. *(Jack Brown collection)*

RIGHT: A close-up of one of the Velle 'Shipshape' cranes fitted to the **Menelaus**, showing the system of steel ropes and pulleys for raising, lowering and swinging the boom. *(Jack Brown collection)*

ABOVE: The Blue Funnel Line's *Memnon* at sea, shortly after completion by Mitsubishi Heavy Industries in 1977. *(Jack Brown collection)*

The vehicle decks on the 'Super Vikings' were arranged similarly to those of the most recent Sealink ferries with two longitudinal casings dividing the space into three sections. As with the *Hengist*, *Horsa* and *Senlac*, a system of platforms giving complete or various degrees of coverage was specified – but James Ayers was concerned that raising and lowering these regularly by winding in and paying out steel rope would lead to fatigue and ongoing maintenance problems. Brown therefore devised a more robust alternative solution; this was to move each platform using direct-acting hydraulic cylinders. Operating in pairs, the tops of the cylinders were attached to the platforms and accommodated in recesses in the casings while the ends of the pistons were attached to the deckhead. Lowering and raising the platform panels was accomplished by novel hydraulic circuitry, which included oil delivery to and from the cylinders through holes drilled

through the lengths of the piston rods, thereby avoiding any need for flexible hydraulic pipes. As with the *Vortigern*, the 'Super Vikings' had an additional upper car deck, filling the aft third of Main Deck in the superstructure. When bow-in, this was accessed via a ramp, lowered to the platform deck and, when stern-in, cars drove over the aft mooring deck.

In service, the 'Super Vikings' proved to be highly effective and popular vessels and, although they were not used on the Dover Strait as had been expected, they proved their worth on routes from Portsmouth and between Felixstowe and Zeebrugge.

While the 'Super Vikings' were being built in Aalborg, in the Bremerhaven shipyard of Schichau Unterweser A.G., a class of three innovative freight ferries for operation across Townsend Thoresen's route network, including the high-intensity Dover Strait services, was constructed.

RIGHT: A sectional profile drawing showing the configuration of the Cargospeed Velle cranes on the M-class cargo liners and these vessels' ability to carry containers and general cargo. *(Jack Brown collection)*

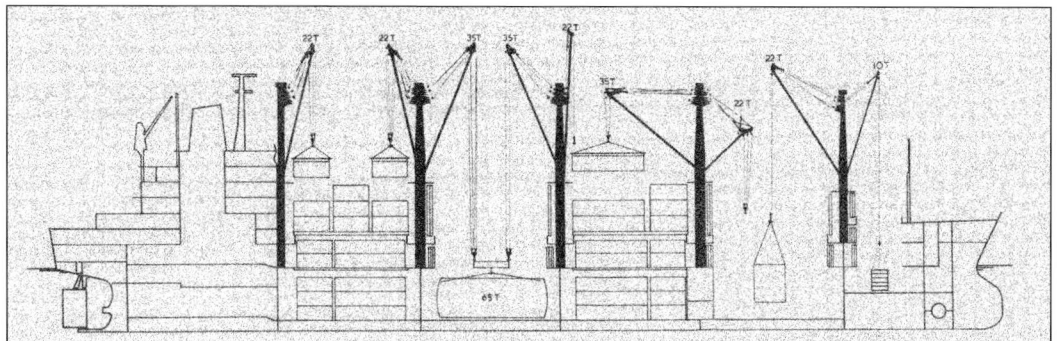

Designed by James Ayers, the 3,335gt *European Trader*, *European Gateway* and *European Clearway* of 1975-77 were actually the first of their type to offer simultaneous drive-through loading and unloading on two deck levels. The vessels had similar ramp arrangements to the 'Super Vikings' in that the outer section of the bow ramp could be removed by the visor to fit at French and Belgian ports on the Dover Strait. To enable vehicles to access the upper vehicle deck by crossing the bow mooring deck, the visor was on very long arms so that, when opened, it was held high in the air with enough space for trucks to drive beneath.

While the equipment needed by Townsend Thoresen was being made, Cargospeed also fulfilled a contract received from the Belgian State-owned Regie voor Maritiem Transport. This was supply doors, ramps and platform decks for the 5,635gt Oostende-Dover ferries *Prinses Marie Christine* and *Prinses Maria Esmeralda*, built by Cockerill's shipyard at Hoboken and completed in 1975. Unusually, the stern door was in two vertical sections, which slid on rollers to close in a V-shaped configuration. These were heavy and therefore required to be robustly secured to prevent any risk of them sliding open at sea, as

had happened with disastrous consequences on the nearly new Norwegian ferry *Skagerrak* in September 1966. She was inundated via the stern and sank off the Danish coast. On the new Belgian ferries, Brown specified the 'Autocleat' system previously developed for the shell doors and internal bulkhead doors on the paper and car carriers *Laurentian Forest* and *Avon Forest*. The sequentially engaged cleating around the edges of both door panels would hold them firmly in position, no matter how far the ferries rolled from side to side.

The Cockerill yard's drawing office designed the hulls' side web frames with large radius 'beam-knees' connecting to the deckhead beams, and this made the stowage of platform decks very difficult as the knees would prevent them from being fully hoisted. The solution was to design small hinged panels on each platform deck panel where it would meet a web frame. These would fold down before the panels were fully raised and, when lowered, would be hinged up by little stalks landing on the stringers (i.e. the horizontal framing inside the shell plating at mezzanine deck level).

The period from the mid-1970s onwards was a bleak one for Scottish manufacturing businesses

ABOVE: The SD14-type cargo vessel *Bronte*, completed in 1979 by Austin & Pickersgill in Sunderland for Lamport & Holt of Liverpool, was one of many examples of this standard ship type equipped by Cargospeed with Velle 'Shipshape' cranes. She operated relatively briefly in liner service between UK and South American ports as her route was soon given over to fully containerised tonnage. *(Jack Brown collection)*

BELOW: The unique 10,328gt SD15 cargo liner *Armadale*, built by Austin & Pickersgill Ltd in 1970 for Trinder, Anderson & Company Ltd, of London and equipped with Cargospeed Velle cranes and hatch covers. *(Jack Brown collection)*

ABOVE: The 1972-built cargo liner *Orbita* was delivered in 1972 from Cammell Laird of Birkenhead to the Pacific Steam Navigation Co. As can be seen in this stern-quarter aerial view, her hull is arranged with twinned hatches, divided along the centre line by a stiffening member. The arrangement was typical of such vessels in the latter 1960s and early 1970s. Velle 'Shipshape' cranes are also installed. *(Jack Brown collection)*

LEFT & RIGHT The *Orbita* with Cargospeed Velle cranes working cargo. *(Jack Brown collection)*

and both Cargospeed and George Brown & Co. experienced the difficulties faced by the heavy industrial sector as a whole. In the wake of the Oil Crisis, Jim Callaghan's Labour Government presided over a period of barely controlled inflation (which at one point hit 28 per cent). In such a climate, the unpredictability of future labour and materials costs made it very difficult to price contracts with any degree of accuracy. The Government's solution to the high inflation was to

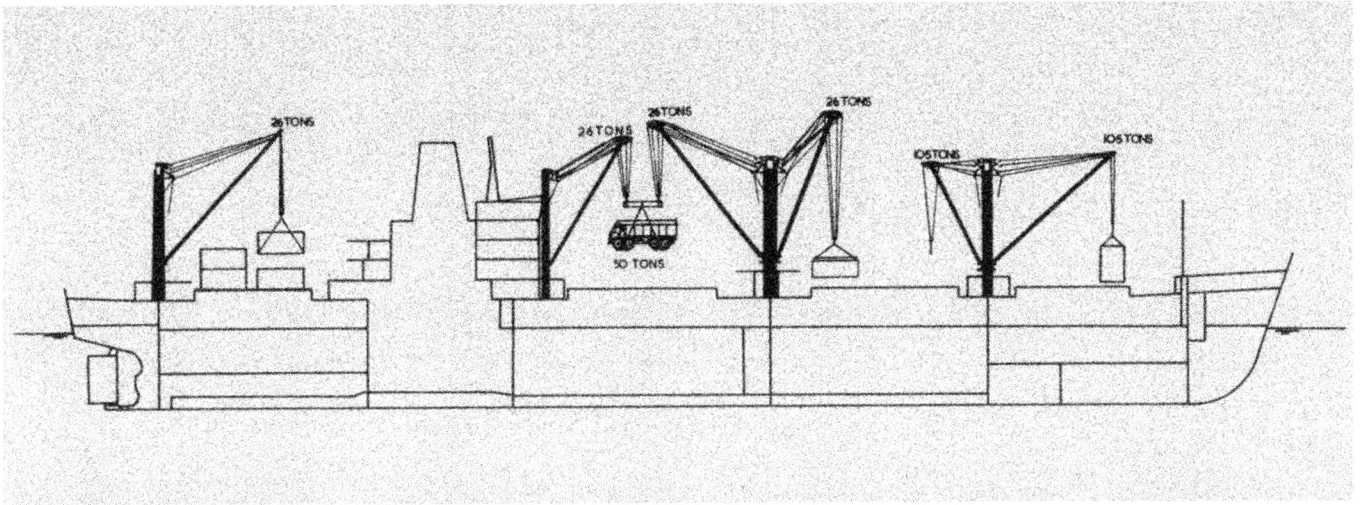

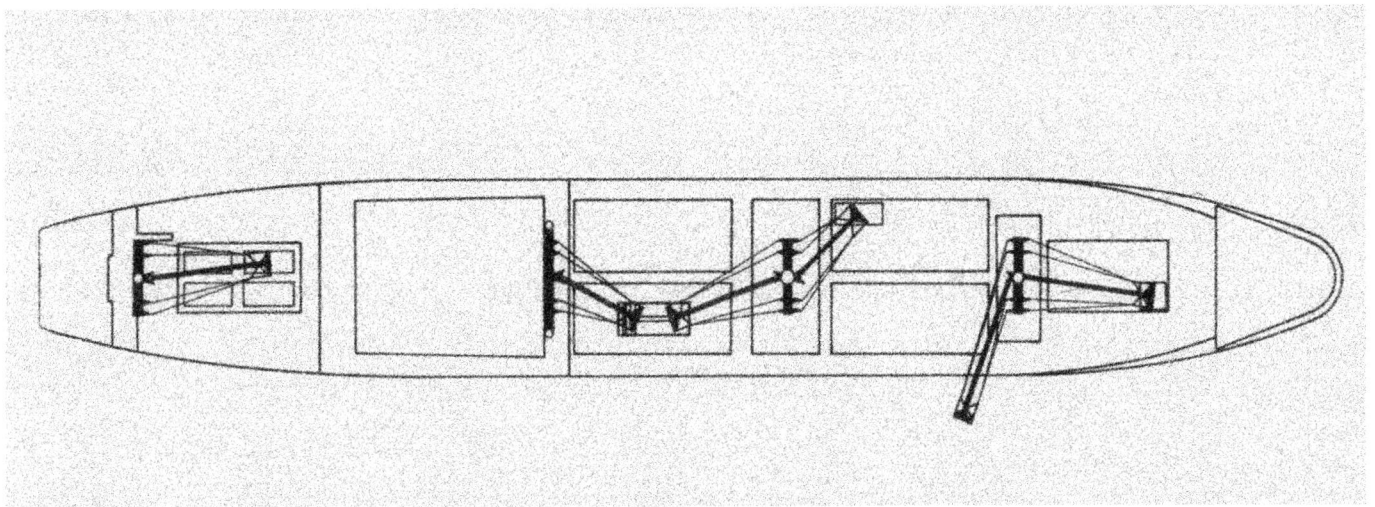

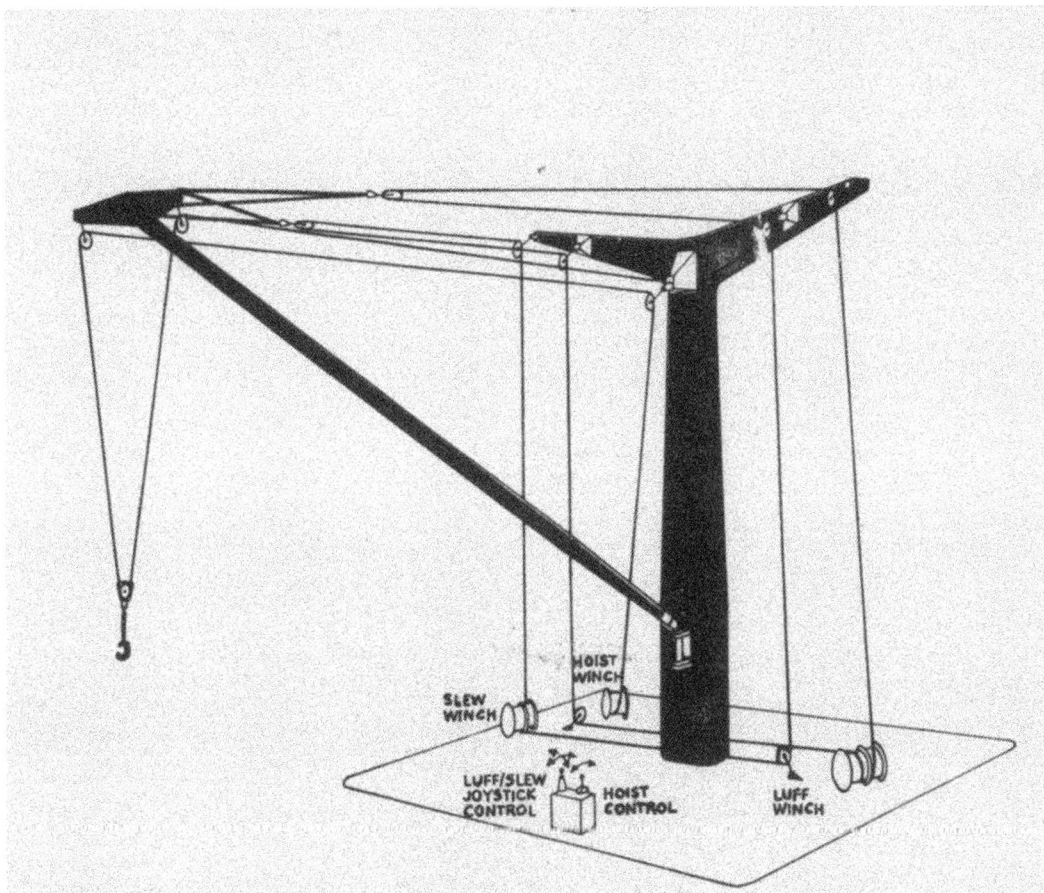

The Orbita with Cargospeed Velle cranes working cargo.

TOP & CENTRE: A sectional profile drawing and plan drawing showing the configuration of the Cargospeed Velle cranes on the *Orbita* and on her sisterships *Orduna* and *Ortega*. (Jack Brown collection)

LEFT: A diagram of the Velle 'Shipshape' crane rigging; showing how ropes were simultaneously paid out and wound in on split-barrel winches; on the luffing winch, both ropes wound in or paid out together and on the slewing winch one rope wound in as the other paid out. (Jack Brown collection)

ABOVE: The Bank Line (Andrew Weir Shipping) cargo liner *Tenchbank* was one of a series of six built by Sunderland Shipbuilders Ltd in 1979 for round-the-world service and fitted with Cargospeed Velle 'Shipshape' cranes. *(Jack Brown collection)*

raise interest rates sharply and this strengthened the pound to such an extent that it became hard to win export orders with a decent profit margin. Besides, fixed-price contracts were standard practice in the shipbuilding supply sector, meaning that there was no margin for subsequent

adjustment to take account of currency and inflationary fluctuations.

Typical Cargospeed contracts specified that a 10 per cent deposit should be paid upon signature, 25 per cent three months before delivery, 60 per cent upon delivery and 5 per cent

ABOVE: The *Badagry Palm*, operated by Ocean Transport & Trading Ltd's Palm Line subsidiary, was likewise built in 1979 by Sunderland Shipbuilders Ltd. *(Jack Brown collection)*

upon completion and successful installation. As British shipyards were also struggling to cope with the era's macro-economic pressures, Brown frequently found it was necessary personally to 'chase' them for instalment payments. Yet, George Brown & Co.'s 80-strong workforce still required to be paid every Friday evening.

In 1973, a new manager had been appointed to Royal Bank of Scotland's Greenock branch, which held the George Brown & Co. and Cargospeed accounts and, due to his extreme parsimony, the traditionally cordial relationship between the bank and the companies declined. Requests for overdrafts were refused, and

ABOVE: Caledonian MacBrayne's Gourock-Dunoon cross-Clyde car ferry ***Juno*** is seen off Gourock shortly after entering service in 1975. *(A. Ernest Glen)*

BELOW: The combined mechanism on the ***Jupiter*** and ***Juno***, cushioning the ramp closure, latching it secure and pushing out on lowering. *(Jack Brown collection)*

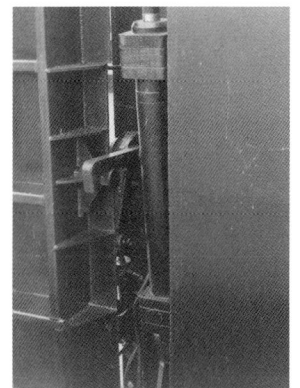

LEFT: The Southampton-Cowes ferry ***Netley Castle*** crosses the Solent in the latter-1970s. Built by Ryton Marine Ltd of Wallsend on Tyne, she was fitted with Cargospeed ramps and elevating platform decks. *(Bruce Peter collection)*

RIGHT: The launching of the *Jupiter* at James Lamont & Co's Port Glasgow shipyard in November 1973. (*A. Ernest Glen*)

LEFT: A Leyland truck drives off the recently-introduced *Netley Castle* at Southampton at the end of a crossing from the Isle of Wight. Note the relatively steep angle of descent down the Cargospeed ramp at high tide. (*Jack Brown collection*)

RIGHT: The *Netley Castle* vehicle deck with four hoistable ramp panels which, when lowered, became car decks allowing one lane of freight and five lanes of cars to be transported (*Jack Brown collection*)

RIGHT: A stern-quarter view of the Scrabster-Stromness ferry *St Ola*, built in 1974 by Hall Russell & Co Ltd of Aberdeen and fitted with Cargospeed bow and stern doors, platform decks and a car elevator. (*Ferry Publications Library*)

ABOVE: The Canadian Great Lakes ferry ***Chi-Cheemaun*** of 1974 was constructed by Collingwood Shipyards in Ontario for operation between Tobermory and South Baymouth on Manitoulin Island in Lake Superior. Note the vessel's slender bow lines, necessitating an unusually large visor. *(Jack Brown collection)*

LEFT: The ***Chi-Cheemaun***, shown nearing completion at Collingwood Shipyards with her large bow visor raised and the access ramp lowered. *(Jack Brown collection)*

RIGHT: The top-hinged stern door on the ***Chi-Cheemaun***. *(Jack Brown collection)*

LEFT: Townsend Thoresen's Aalborg built Channel ferry ***Viking Viscount*** at Felixstowe at the end of another crossing from Zeebrugge. Vehicles simultaneously unloading from Upper and Main deck levels. *(Miles Cowsill)*

ABOVE: The St Lawrence Seaway ferry *Camille Marcoux*, built in 1974 by Marine Industrie Ltd of Sorel in Quebec and featuring Cargospeed bow and stern doors and elevating platform decks. *(Jack Brown collection)*

RIGHT: The freight ferry *Dundalk* was a product of the Verolme Cork Dockyard and operated by the British & Irish Steam Packet Company, carrying trucks, trailers and containers. She was equipped with Cargospeed bow and stern doors. *(Bruce Peter collection)*

BELOW LEFT & RIGHT: The 7,892gt rail freight and trailer ferry Incan ***Incan St Laurent*** was built in 1975 by Burrard Dry Dock Co. for Incan Ships Ltd of Montreal, a joint venture between the Canadian Pacific Railroad and the Inchcape Group of London. Intended for operation in Quebec, she was chartered instead for Alaskan coastal service and eventually sold to Canadian National. She was equipped with a large Cargospeed 'Autocleat' stern door. *(Jack Brown collection)*

guarantees for existing overdrafts were demanded. Upon being told suddenly by the bank manager 'not to write any more cheques', a meeting at the bank's Edinburgh head office was quickly arranged. At the meeting, it was emphasised that foreclosure of George Brown & Co. and Cargospeed would cause severe problems for Royal Bank of Scotland's subsidiary William & Glynn, based in London. Cargospeed had for some years been using William & Glynn's

RIGHT: Large numbers of passengers on deck enjoy summer evening sunlight as Townsend Thoresen's Aalborg built Channel ferry **Viking Valiant** nears the end of another crossing of the Western Channel from France. *(Bruce Peter collection)*

BELOW: Four diagrams showing the stern and bow openings of the 'Super Vikings'. The two upper images show the extended stern door/ramp and the full length bow ramp; and the two lower images show the divided stern door and the shortened bow ramp achieved by the outer part attached to the inside of the bow visor. *(Jack Brown collection)*

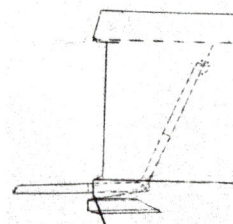

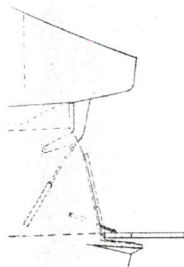

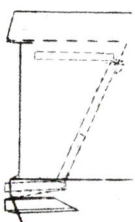

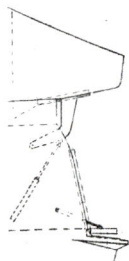

forward foreign exchange department, which ensured predictable forward exchange rates. At the time, Cargospeed had many forward exchange contracts directly with William & Glynn for tens of millions of Danish kroner (relating to the 'Super Viking' contracts with Aalborg Værft) and deutschmarks (for the Schichau Unterweser contracts). These William & Glynn foreign exchange contracts were unknown to the local manager, but were clearly known to Edinburgh head office who lifted the cheque-writing embargo. For Cargospeed's management, this came as a considerable relief – but the incident nonetheless illustrates the severe difficulties faced by traditional British manufacturers in the era.

The unfriendly local bank manager had been required to take a more constructive approach but was replaced in the late 1970s by another mean incumbent who, according to Brown, pushed several well-known Greenock-based companies into liquidation during the latter 1970s. Indeed, by 1980, only George Brown & Co. and

Black's, a manufacturer of camping equipment, remained as major employers where management decisions were made locally. (Other Greenock companies – such as Kincaid's and British Shipbuilders – were headquartered elsewhere.)

In the latter 1970s orders were fewer due in part to a lull in the wake of another Oil Crisis in 1978 and Britain's high inflation. One minor project was to provide the stern ramp for a new Caledonian MacBrayne Wemyss Bay-Rothesay ferry, the 851gt *Saturn*, completed in 1978 by Ailsa Shipbuilding at Troon as a follow-up to the successful *Jupiter* and *Juno*. A more substantial repeat order was for Regie voor Maritiem Transport's 6,019gt *Prins Albert*, a near-sister of the *Prinses Marie Christine* and *Prinses Maria Esmeralda* and likewise built by Cockerill's of Hoboken. Another significant contract was to design and manufacture doors and hoistable platform decks for a new B&I Line passenger and vehicle ferry, the 6,796gt *Connacht*, built by Verolme Cork Dockyard for the Liverpool-Dublin

RIGHT: View through the open side-hinged inner bow doors towards the stowed bow ramp on one of the 'Super Vikings'. *(Jack Brown collection)*

ABOVE: The *European Clearway*'s two-part Cargospeed stern door, the lower third of which could be disconnected from the upper two thirds to meet linkspans at Channel ports with the upper part being retracted into the deck-head. At ports requiring ramp access, the entire door could be lowered as a single piece. *(Jack Brown collection)*

TOP RIGHT: A shore-based hinged loading ramp, lowered to give direct access to the *European Clearway*'s stern mooring deck, across which vehicles could access her upper freight deck. *(Jack Brown collection)*

RIGHT: The same procedure at the bow, where the visor was mounted on long arms. (*(Jack Brown collection)*

BELOW: The *European Clearway*, berthed stern-in at a double-deck linkspan at Dover. *(Jack Brown collection)*

RIGHT: Shown at Dover shortly after having entered service in 1976, Townsend Thoresen's double-deck freight ferry *European Clearway* featured Cargospeed bow and stern doors and a superstructure forward door. *(Ferry Publications Library)*

RIGHT: Shown at Dover shortly after having entered service in 1976, Townsend Thoresen's double-deck freight ferry *European Clearway* featured Cargospeed bow and stern doors and a superstructure forward door. *(Ferry Publications Library)*

and Holyhead-Dublin routes; she entered service in 1979. For the British Government, top-hinged watertight doors were supplied for the large 20,043gt Royal Fleet Auxiliary supply ships *Fort* *Grange* and *Fort Austin*, delivered in 1978 and 1979 respectively from Scott's Shipbuilding in Greenock. (These projects were similar in scope to the mid-1960s-built *Lyness*, *Stromness* and *Torbarness*.)

LEFT: The *Prinses Maria-Esmeralde*'s open bow visor with shipyard workers completing her watertight inner doors, which retracted into the shell plating on either side of the opening. Note the large amount of space between the visor and inner door – a classification requirement for high safety margin. Visible is the hatch cover forward of the bridge which was included in the comprehensive ro-ro access equipment supplied by Cargospeed. *(Jack Brown collection)*

RIGHT: The *Prinses Maria-Esmeralde*'s stern, with Cargospeed 'Autocleat' side-rolling doors opened to Port and Starboard. *(Jack Brown collection)*

RIGHT The *Prinses Maria-Esmeralde* en route between Dover and Ostend. *(Miles Cowsill)*

An unusual contract won by Cargospeed in 1978 was to design and supply a travelling gantry especially for the lifting from afloat of 107-tonne Boeing Jetfoil fast ferries in the Venezuelan Coracrevi Marina. This large fabrication by George Brown & Co. incorporated several notable features, including a long shaft fitted with four separate winch drums and powered by two of the largest Hagglunds hydraulic motors. Following overload testing, the gantry was despatched to Venezuela to enable the servicing of Jetfoils operating to the large offshore island of Margarita.

While George Brown & Co.'s production equipment had been kept up to date with multiple overhead cranes, an automatic boom welder, programmable flame burning gear and many additional tools in the machine shop – which had tripled in size since the mid-1960s – the corrugated steel exteriors of the fabrication sheds were rusted and looking decrepit. The ground in

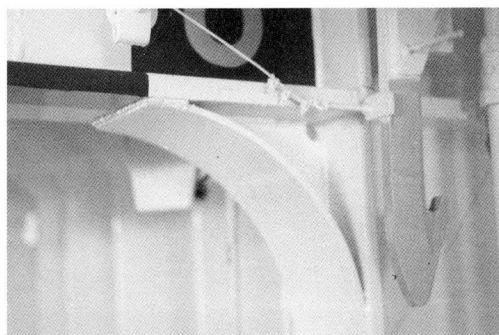

LEFT: Small hinged flaps at the corners of the hoistable platform deck panels on the **Prinses Marie Christine** and **Prinses Maria-Esmeralde** enabled the panels to be hoisted up between the curved beam-knees where the web-frames connected to the transverse beams. Small stalks landing on the horizontal shell stringer, at platform deck level, hinged the flaps up. *(Jack Brown collection)*

LEFT: The same space with the Cargospeed 'Autocleat' stern doors closed ready to put to sea. Note the curved beam-knees where the hull shell web-frames connect with the transverse beams at the deck-head. *(Jack Brown collection)*

LEFT: The Belgian RMT Channel ferry **Prins Albert** of 1978, a near-sister of the Prinses Marie Christine and Prinses Maria-Esmarelda. *(Bruce Peter collection)*

the areas of the old shipbuilding berths was bare compacted earth and there was an accumulation of discarded cut-offs of steel and rivets that had corroded together as a mass of industrial waste. There was sadly too little money available to invest in non-essential items or better infrastructure. In complete contrast, Navire Oy in Finland, one of Cargospeed's two key rivals in the manufacture of cranes, hatch covers and ro-ro access equipment, had a brand new state-of-the-art factory at Naantali, completed in 1975 at which components were assembled on production lines and, upon completion, were loaded on specialist vessels at a purpose-built quay to be sailed to whichever shipyard had ordered them. In comparison with such an up-to-date industrial environment, Cargospeed equipment was made under sub-optimal conditions.

Jack Brown recalls that at a trade exhibition in 1966 Henri Kummerman the President of the MacGregor organisation had tried to persuade him to sell Cargospeed. Kummerman offered Brown the position of International Director for Research and Development, but he had no interest whatsoever in the George Brown & Co. shipyard. Brown, however, felt loyalty to the employees there and decided to reject Kummerman's offer in order to continue manufacturing in Greenock.

To give continuity to George Brown & Co., Brown's major hope was for Cargospeed soon to win contracts to manufacture ro-ro access and vehicle deck equipment for an expected new generation of British Rail ferries to replace the remaining steam turbine vessels by 1980. In 1976, Jack Brown was contacted by Tony Rogan and Don Ripley of British Rail who were preparing designs for new Sealink Dover-Calais ferries which, as with Townsend Thoresen's 'European'

RIGHT: A stern-quarter view of the **Saturn**, showing her Cargospeed stern- and side vehicle access ramps. *(Jack Brown collection)*

LEFT: Lowering the stern ramp on the **Saturn** at the Wemyss Bay linkspan and a car driving off. *(Jack Brown collection)*

class freighters, would provide for drive-through loading simultaneously on both upper and lower vehicle decks. British Rail additionally wanted the vessels to be capable of loading both decks from only the lower level and, to enable this to happen sufficiently quickly, Brown suggested that the best way would be to fabricate the entire superstructure-enclosed upper vehicle deck in the form of a vast ramp which could be hinged down from either the forward or the aft ends. A significant benefit of the arrangement would be the very easy gradients and the capability to raise the fully loaded ramp for securing at upper deck level. Brown named this design 'Tiltdek'. Don Ripley had another idea which was the formation of four large ramps, two hinging down aft and two hinging down forward from a short length of permanent upper deck at midships.

After nearly three years' preparatory work, in 1979, British Rail ordered four examples of the new ferry type from Harland & Wolff's Belfast shipyard – the 6,630gt *Galloway Princess* for service between Stranraer and Larne, the 7,197gt *St David* for the Holyhead-Dun Laoghaire route and the 7,003gt *St Anselm* and *St Christopher* for Dover-Calais, which had become Sealink's premier Channel ferry route. Unfortunately for Cargospeed, who had quoted to build the large ramps as well as bow and stern doors, the order was awarded to MacGregor.

Fortunately for Cargospeed, at this point, Sealink's rival, Townsend Thoresen, discovered what was afoot and felt obliged to respond urgently as the new railway-owned ferries would threaten its market lead on the Dover-Calais service. Townsend Thoresen's in-house naval architect James Ayers argued that the best

solution would be to construct three identical fast 8,000gt double-deck ferries. A high freight capacity would be vital to the success of his proposed business model because hovercraft and, eventually, the Channel Tunnel would cream off more of the passenger market.

In designing the vessels, Ayers sought to combine a fast speed with a high deadweight capacity, enabling typical crossings of only 75 minutes' duration (as opposed to Sealink's hour-and-a-half timings). Ayers briefed Brown that each ferry would make six return trips a day, 50 weeks a year for at least 20 years and so whatever equipment Cargospeed supplied would need to be very robust and reliable.

A major innovation was Brown's new design for the bow and stern doors, which he called 'Neatstow'. Unlike the lifting visors on all previous ferries with Cargospeed equipment, these would open out and sideways in a 'distorted parallelogram' action without protruding beyond the belting. This offered both safety and operational enhancements as, unlike ferries with visors, there would be neither upward wave pressure nor the risk of damage during berthing procedures due to the belting's protection. Moving such large steel structures quickly, reliably and without straining any part of the structure would not be simple. The doors were hinged on very substantial arms, supporting their entire weight. These swung the doors out while separate link-arms kept them on trajectories to open positions parallel with the shell casings. To ensure a smooth action, the underside of the doors had a spring-loaded wheel which ran on the top surface of the belting. Each door locked with three vertical pins at the top and three at the

RIGHT: Caledonian MacBrayne's Wemyss Bay-Rothesay ferry **Saturn**, which entered service across the Clyde in 1978. *(Jack Brown collection)*

bottom, and they were held together with over-centre cleats. At the bow, an inner pair of watertight doors hinged apart to open positions against the inner side casings.

Townsend Thoresen was fortunate that the builder, Schichau Unterweser in Bremerhaven, was able to construct each 7,951gt ferry in only a year, meaning that the first, named the *Spirit of Free Enterprise*, was completed in January 1980, nine months ahead of British Rail's *St Anselm*. (All four vessels' building in Belfast suffered protracted delays due to various supply and labour problems at Harland & Wolff's yard.) The *Herald of Free Enterprise* and the *Pride of Free Enterprise* followed shortly thereafter.

Having failed to win the British Rail contracts, Jack Brown was determined to win the Townsend Thoresen order and so a very competitive tender in deutschmarks was submitted to Schichau Unterweser. Cargospeed was successful in tendering for all three vessels – but because it was necessary to meet a very tight delivery deadline for the *Spirit of Free Enterprise*, George Brown & Co. needed to subcontract some of the manufacture to other steel fabricators. Partly because of this and partly due to ongoing high interest rates in Britain, George Brown & Co. lost some £100,000 fulfilling the contract. The subsequent deliveries for *Herald of Free Enterprise* and *Pride of Free Enterprise* were

successful and achieved at least small profit margins.

With a keen eye for new opportunities, in 1978 Jack Brown had established a new company, Videowest Services Ltd, to use the newly emerging video recording technology to make promotional films for industry. Another potential role was to supply closed-circuit television and recording equipment for ferry vehicle decks and wherever else it might be needed. He tried to interest Townsend Thoresen's naval architects in specifying an installation on the vehicle decks of their new ferries but was told 'our existing systems are fail-safe, Mr Brown. One man closes the doors and another man checks that the doors are closed.'

In March 1987, the *Herald of Free Enterprise* was deputising on the Dover-Zeebrugge service. On the evening of the 6th, the ferry left the berth in Zeebrugge with her bow doors open and headed out to sea. As there was a high tide, she

LEFT: The *Connacht*'s open bow visor. (*Jack Brown collection*)

BELOW: The port-side hydraulic stern door operating cylinder with the door hinged open. (*Jack Brown collection*)

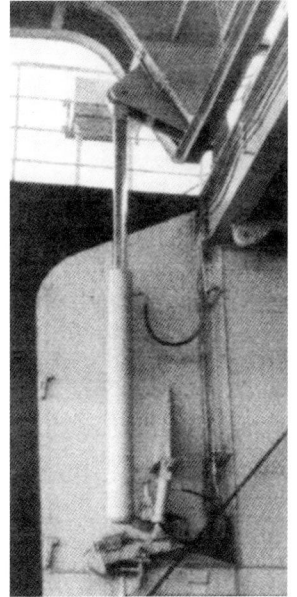

LEFT & RIGHT: Usually, centre casings provide lateral support for platform decks and hoistable ramps but, as the *Connacht*'s decks were full width for part of the vessel's length, this was not possible. The solution was a special folding frame which lowered with the ramp from the deck head. (*Jack Brown collection*)

BELOW: Inside part of *Connacht*'s vehicle deck, showing the shell on the left and the centreline casing on the right with elevating platform deck lowered. (*Jack Brown collection*)

TOP LEFT & RIGHT: In 1976, the Greek Adelphi Vergottis-owned roll-on, roll-off freight ferries **Farha** and **Bahjah** were rebuilt with a novel arrangement of trailer lift from Main Deck to tank-top level, whereby both the lift platform and the Main Deck hatch cover were combined into one structure. The top left image shows the equipment for one of the vessels under fabrication at the Garvel Shipyard. The top right image was taken at Perama where it was being installed. Unusually, the elevator was operated by a single direct-acting cylinder at mid-length with all out-of-balance forces being absorbed by guide rollers engaged in vertical shipside tracks. *(Jack Brown collection)*

LEFT: The hydraulic power pack, manufactured at Garvel Shipyard, to operate the elevator. *(Jack Brown collection)*

CENTRE RIGHT: A diagram showing the operation of the elevator with the hydraulic cylinder and tracked guide wheels. *(Jack Brown collection)*

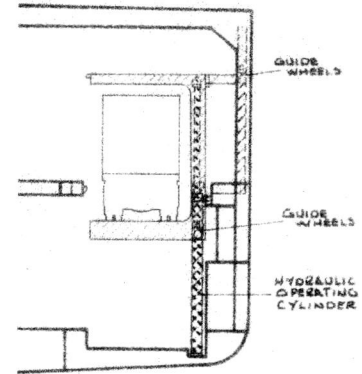

LOWER LEFT & RIGHT: Cargospeed Velle hatch covers on the Harrisons (Clyde) Ltd bulk carrier **Volnay**, built in 1969 by John Brown & Co. Ltd shortly after the Queen Elizabeth 2; this very extensive installation was a lucrative contract for Cargospeed. I*(Jack Brown collection)*

BOTTOM: The **Islander,** built in 1969 by John Lewis & Sons Ltd of Aberdeen for the Orkney Isles Shipping Company, was fitted with standard Velle hatch covers on coaming aft and flush-fitting covers forward, plus a 'gullwing' shell door for livestock access all by Cargospeed. *(Jack Brown collection)*

Velle 'Shipshape' cranes were installed on a series of circa 13,200gt bulk carriers built by Lithgows Ltd of Port Glasgow for Kr Jebsens Rederi A/S of Bergen between 1969 and 1970; these were the **Baugnes**, **Baknes**, **Bulknes**, **Brooknes**, **Binsnes** and **Blidnes**. Four-rope grabbing was developed by Cargospeed for these vessels. The top-right image is of **Baugnes** discharging sulphur in the port of Esperance, Western Australia. The small left hand image shows a model at the Garvel Shipyard, showing the system being demonstrated to the satisfaction of Jebsens' management. The small right image shows the grab closing. *(Jack Brown collection)*

LEFT: The roll-on, roll-off freight ferry **Caribbean Endeavour**, shown berthed in Miami, was rebuilt in 1979 with an additional forward-located external vehicle deck, designed by Cargospeed. *(Jack Brown collection)*

RIGHT: The container feeder ship **Wicklow,** built in 1971 by Verolme Cork Dockyard for the British & Irish Steam Packet Company, was fitted with a combination of Cargospeed Velle folding hatch covers and 'piggyback' longitudinally rolling hatch covers. While one hatch panel rolled back, another 'piggybacked' on top of it. *(Jack Brown collection)*

Garvel Shipyard Activities

TOP LEFT: The fabrication of hatch covers for the Harrisons (Clyde) Ltd bulk carrier **Volnay** in the latter 1960s. *(Jack Brown collection)*

TOP RIGHT: Hatch cover and mast constructions in progress. *(Jack Brown collection)*

UPPER MIDDLE LEFT AND RIGHT: 'Velle 'Shipshape' crane masts and crosstrees in process of fabrication. *(Jack Brown collection)*

LOWER MIDDLE LEFT: A mid-1970s Cargospeed designed gantry crane framework for the lifting from afloat of Boeing 'Jetfoil' ferries. *(Jack Brown collection)*

LOWER MIDDLE RIGHT: The hull of the Mexican buoy maintenance vessel **Aries** in the largest fabrication shed at Garvel Shipyard. *(Jack Brown collection)*

BOTTOM LEFT: The Garvel Shipyard machine shop as it appeared in the early 1970s. *(Jack Brown collection)*

BOTTOM RIGHT UPPER: A 'Neatstow' stern door panel for the Townsend Thoresen Dover Straits ferry **Spirit of Free Enterprise** ready for delivery from Garvel. *(Jack Brown collection)*

BOTTOM RIGHT: A mixture of Velle 'Shipshape' crane fittings being processed in the machine shop. *(Jack Brown collection)*

The **Lancashire Coast**, which had been built by George Brown & Co. in 1954 as the **Ulster Pioneer**, is shown undergoing conversion in the James Watt Dock in Greenock in 1967. The vessel was retrofitted with Velle hydraulically operated hatch covers; an internal ramp, and a 'Gull-Wing' side door. *(Jack Brown collection)*

"TILTDEK" was originally proposed for a British Rail Sealink project in 1978 as a system whereby the entire useable Upper Deck garage area could be sloped , or tilted, to permit direct vehicle access to/from lanes without manoeuvring. Elevator access space loss is avoided, and ferry turnround times shortened.

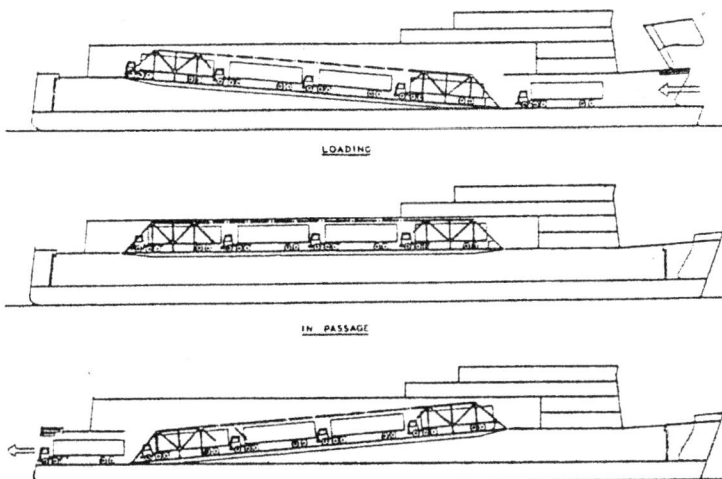

LOADING

IN PASSAGE

In it's original form, "TILTDEK" was developed as a lattice girder bridge structure of some 65 metres length.

LEFT: Intended as a possibility for British Rail's early-1980s Dover-Calais ferries, 'Tiltdek' was one of Jack Brown's many patents. *(Jack Brown collection)*

Patents

896352	"Finger platform" for pallet operations	1333169	Ramp through W.T. bulkhead
		1380416	"Autocleat" door cleating
997029	Stern door operation	1388658	Elevator vertical hoist drum winch
999708	Load stabilizing rig for Velle crane	1389658	"Trio" ramps
1009737	"Self-levelling platform"	1411939	"Contoffon" crane
1013570	Hatch cover actuator	1438755	"Curved Tidebridge"
1014691	3 stage ramp system	1520271	"Rotatable Tidebridge"
1015741	Self-grading ramp	1524962	Elevator "L-evator"
1025074	TV monitoring	1537270	Dover gangway
1050039	Slotted bridle for Velle crane	1569564	"Portafloat"
1067016	Cantilever hatch covers	1567756	Propulsion modules
1094281	Balanced stern door	1599837	"Switchtail Tidebridge"
1097351	"Autobeam" hatch covers	2009054	"Tiltdek" hydr ram ops
1100691	"Gradient" hatch covers	2021488	"Tiltdeck" rope ops
1110272	Liferaft launching davit	2022517	'ROROBOW"
1157781	"Doorman crane"	2047310	"Neatstow" bow and stern doors
1169101	"Lowstow" hatch covers	2053100	"Floating Tidebridge"
1205862	Ferry car decks	2061191	"Rail switchevator"
1244865	Container gate	2071021	"Intraface ramp"
1249320	Overlap hatch covers	2081350	"Rail Tidebridge"
1287757	Hatch covers ram actuators	2086821	St.Lawrence Seaway propulsion modules
1299364	Double shell door		
1300222	Roll round conveyor		
1331741	Original curved ramps		

Cargospeed and its parent Company George Brown & Co. (Marine) Ltd. at Garvel Shipyard have experienced difficult times in 1974 and 1975 due to unforeseeable levels of inflation affecting fixed price orders booked prior to the fourfold oil price "hike" late 1973. To use Mr. Brown's words "it has been a rough ride but we are still in our saddles". Despite the difficulties, Cargospeed has delivered equipment to 33 vessels during 1974 and 1975, mostly bow and stern doors, car deck systems, and ramp systems for RO-RO ferries built in the U.K., Canada, France, Belguim, Germany, Denmark, Italy, Greece and Australia. Mr. Brown comments that its "certainty that many tens of thousands of Britons will travel on Cargospeed equipped ferries this summer" and mentions that the **Vortigern**, **European Trader**, **European Clearway**, **Holyhead Ferry**, **Chartres**, **St Eloi**, **Princess Maria Esmerelda**, **Prinses Marie Christine** and **Lion** sailing from Dover: the **Hengist** and **Horsa** sailing from Folkestone: the **Senlac** sailing from Newhaven; the **Viking Venturer**, **Viking Valiant** and **Netley Castle** sailing from Southampton;the **Caledonian Princess** sailing from Holyhead; the **Antrim Princess** and **Ailsa Princess** sailing from Stranraer; the **Glen Sannox**, **Juno** and **Jupiter** on Clyde routes; the **Iona** and **Pioneer**, on Western Isle routes; the **St. Ola** on the Stromness-Scrabster route, and the **Viking Voyager**, **Viking Viscount** and **European Gateway** sailing from Felixstowe.

Extract from Greenock Telegraph

ABOVE: Townsend Thoresen's Dover-Calais ferry **Spirit of Free Enterprise** – the first of three highly efficient sisters introduced in 1980 and featuring Cargospeed 'Neatstow' vehicle access doors and elevating platform decks. (*Bruce Peter collection*)

RIGHT: A plan-view, showing the movement of the 'Neatstow' doors fitted to Townsend Thoresen's 'Spirit'-class. (*Jack Brown collection*)

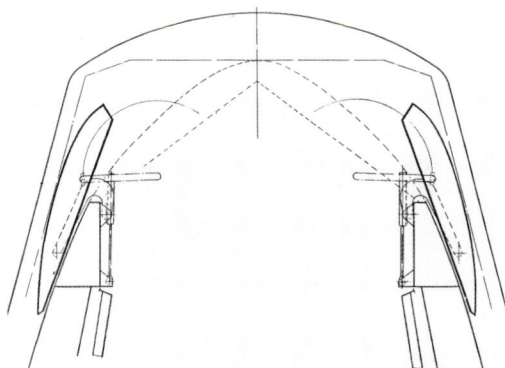

had been trimmed downwards at the bow for vehicle loading and so when her speed increased she began to scoop up increasing quantities of water into her vehicle deck. Just under half an hour from departure, she became critically unstable and capsized, ending up partially submerged, her starboard side resting on a sandbank. Of the 573 passengers on board that evening, 193 drowned as the ferry sank too quickly for her life-saving appliances to be used.

At the public enquiry into the sinking, it was revealed that Townsend Thoresen ferries not infrequently put to sea with their vehicle deck

ABOVE: A stern-quarter view of the newly-completed **Pride of Free Enterprise**, the third of Townsend Thoresen's new trio of vessels. (*Bruce Peter collection*)

LEFT & RIGHT: The bow of the *Spirit of Free Enterprise*, showing her doors in the closed and open positions on the occasion of her maiden call at Dover for berthing trials. (*(Jack Brown collection)*

BELOW: The *Spirit of Free Enterprise*'s stern doors are swung open on substantial hinges; in the wet weather, one can clearly see the track made by the rollers on the door's underside on the ferry's deck. *(Jack Brown collection)*

doors open. Moreover, when the 'Spirit' class vessels had been constructed, the Company's senior management had vetoed the installation of sufficiently powerful trim pumps to ensure that they sailed on an even keel, in order to save a mere £25,000 per ship. Furthermore, Captains had a poor understanding of the deadweight capacity of these vessels and, although the bow doors were just visible from the ends of the bridge wings, there were no indicator lights on the bridge consoles to show whether they had, in fact, been closed. (On the *Herald of Free Enterprise*, the assistant bosun was sleeping in his cabin when he should have been closing the bow doors, and the chief officer whose duty it was to supervise the implementation of correct security procedures on the vehicle deck was on the bridge.) The public enquiry revealed a culture of sloppiness permeating Townsend Thoresen's operations. The Company were aggressively money-minded and

LEFT: A hinge for one of the 'Neatstow' doors for the *Spirit of Free Enterprise* during fabrication at the Gravel Shipyard. *(Jack Brown collection)*

Cargospeed Gallery Deck
and Ramp System

Cargospeed "Neatstow'
Stern Doors

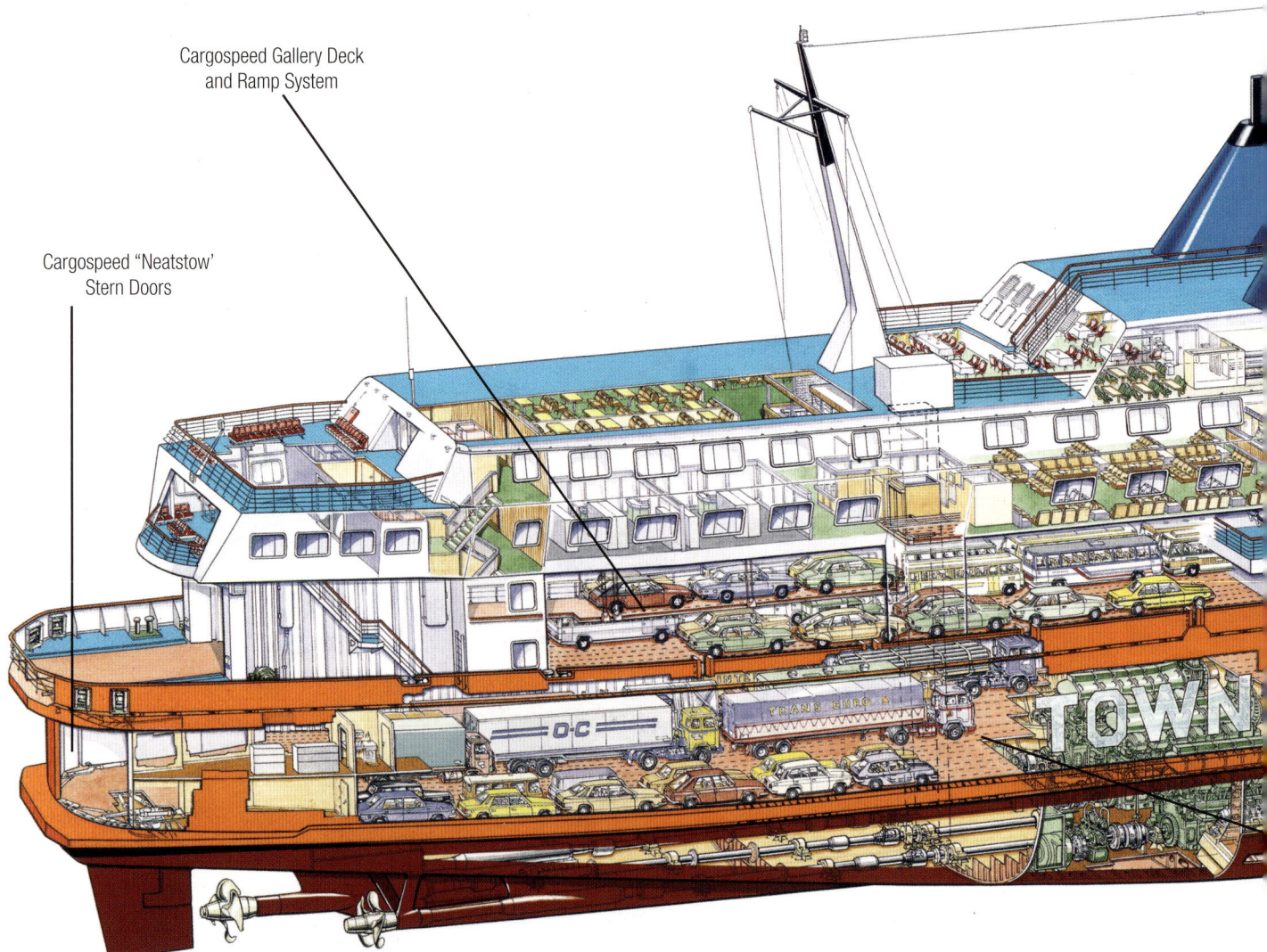

under financial duress, having made unwise property investments in the USA.

Having fulfilled the contracts for the *Spirit of Free Enterprise*, *Herald of Free Enterprise* and *Pride of Free Enterprise* in 1979, Cargospeed received only one further significant order for ferry ro-ro access and vehicle deck equipment. The

6,807gt B&I ferry *Leinster* was a sister to the *Connacht* and likewise built by Verolme Cork Dockyard with delivery in 1981. Fabrication of masts and booms for Velle crane orders was also dwindling and in order to keep George Brown & Co.'s 80-strong workforce employed, Jack Brown decided that the least worse option would be to

RIGHT: A view of the main car deck on the **Spirit of Free Enterprise** . *(Jack Brown collection)*

Cargospeed Bridge Front
Door

Cargospeed Passenger
Access Doors

Cargospeed Inner Bow
Doors

Cargospeed
'Neatstow'
Bow Doors

SPIRIT OF FREE ENTERPRISE

END THORESEN

Vic Berris

Cargospeed Stores Elevator
+ Flush WT Hatch Cover

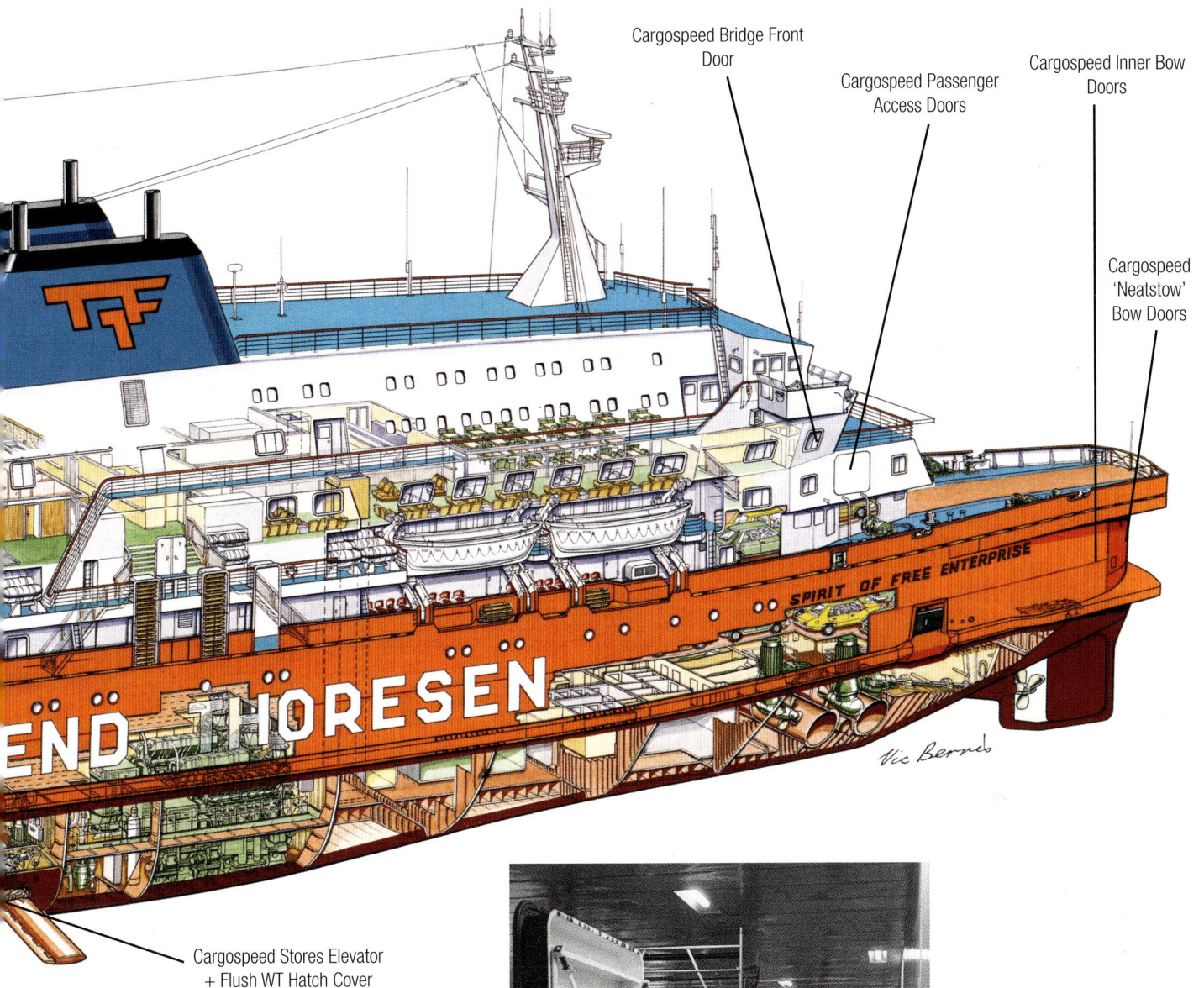

revert to shipbuilding and whatever general steel fabrication work could be found. Since 1962, Brown had often observed that 'the tail is wagging the dog'. By this, he meant that George Brown & Co. was being kept in business by manufacturing cranes, hatches and vehicle access equipment as Cargospeed's subcontractor. Now that George Brown & Co. needed to rely on its own ability to attract orders, Jack Brown and his businesses were in a

ABOVE: 'A highly detailed cut-away drawing showing the layout of Townsend Thoresen's innovative Spirit of Free Enterprise and her two sisters.

Photographs of the vehicle decks access equipment, ramps, elevating platform decks, passenger access doors, and stores hatch/elevators supplied by Cargospeed are appended *(Photographs from Jack Brown's collection)*

SPIRIT OF FREE ENT

LEFT: 'Seen through the doors is the European Trader equipped with specially developed stern and bow doors. *(Jack Brown's collection)*

challenging and unenviable situation.

In 1981-82, two small buoy-handling vessels, the, 146gt *Aries* and *Leo*, were built for the Mexican Government, whose ports of Veracruz on the Caribbean coast and Mazatlan on the Pacific coast hitherto had no such dedicated maintenance vessels. Brown produced the general arrangement plan which included a large Cargospeed deck turntable on which five buoys could be loaded in a circle. A fixed-radius crane was located on the starboard corner of the transom, capable of lifting buoys from the sea over the stern, and lifting them to shore once in port.

The *Aries* was completed successfully and sailed to Veracruz, but while the *Leo* was nearing completion in the late spring of 1982, the Mexican peso became increasingly unstable. Brown considered trying to re-sell the vessel to European

port authorities and re-paying the progress instalments received to date from Mexico. As the orders were partially funded by the British Export Council, there was no other option but to finish the vessel for her original intended owner. Upon completion *Leo* sailed via the Panama Canal to the Pacific, and Brown gave instruction that she be sufficiently fuelled to enable sailing north past Mazatlan to San Diego in California. The night before arrival in Mazatlan, the Mexican peso failed completely and Brown's agents tried – in vain – to instruct the vessel to make for San Diego. The next morning, the *Leo* was berthed in a Mexican naval dockyard, out of reach of any foreign civil authority.

Having fallen out completely with Royal Bank of Scotland, in 1980 Jack Brown had moved his companies' accounts to Bank of Scotland. Its local management was sympathetic to George Brown & Co.'s difficulties and extended a loan equivalent to the value of the final instalment for the *Leo* prior to her departure from Greenock.

In the meantime, George Brown & Co. was building a small Hebridean ferry for the North Uist-Berneray crossing, the 67gt *Eilean Bhearnaraigh*. Her owner was the Shetland Islands Council, which had won the contract to provide this service. Launched in August 1982, she was fitted with a Cargospeed bow ramp and a turntable on deck. Another contract was for a buoy-handling vessel, the 345gt *Wilton*, which was simultaneously under construction for the Tees & Hartlepool Port Authority.

While struggling on with the fabrication of hull 286 (*Wilton*) through September 1982, a further blow struck when George Brown & Co.'s auditors found an error which exacerbated the loss in the previous year's accounts. Combined with the consequences of the Mexican débacle, it became obvious that George Brown & Co. was effectively bankrupt. Tees & Hartlepool were, however, prepared to fund the continuation of the *Wilton*'s construction to the stage of launching, which was accomplished mid-December 1982. Liquidation of George Brown & Co. took place in January 1983 and ended all activities at the Garvel Shipyard

TOP LEFT & RIGHT: The largest Velle 'Shipshape' crane designed and supplied by Cargospeed was installed on the Royal Australian Navy's amphibious landing craft **Tobruk**, built by Carrington Slipways of Tomago, New South Wales and delivered in 1981. The 80-tonne capability enabled complete landing craft to be transferred from deck to afloat and vice-versa. *(Jack Brown collection)*

LEFT & BELOW: This gantry, designed by Cargospeed and manufactured in the late-1970s, was for lifting Boeing 'Jetfoils' for underwater inspection of their foils. Fabricated and overload tested in Greenock, the structure was then dismantled for transport to the port of Puerto la Cruz on Venezuela's north coast. Jetfoils operated from there to the large offshore island of Margarita. *(Jack Brown collection)*

after 82 years. The *Wilton* was Yard Number 286.

In receiving the contract to build the *Wilton*, George Brown & Co. had been required to give the Tees & Hartlepool Port Authority a £70,000 guarantee, provided by a Bristol-based insurance company, which insisted upon a back-to-back guarantee from Jack Brown personally. Brown believed that the guarantee would not be invoked providing the ship was launched on schedule. He was shocked when Tees & Hartlepool had called the guarantee, which left him personally liable for the full amount. Eventually, he managed to pay off this indebtedness.

Jack Brown believed that his other companies – Cargospeed, Videowest and Seaform Design – could continue, but it was then discovered that the companies' accountant had registered them all under the same VAT (Value Added Tax) number. This meant that when George Brown & Co. could not pay its VAT bill, it fell on the other three, bankrupting them as well and so they were liquidated in March-April 1983.

George Brown & Co. had £300,000 of debt – a relatively small sum for a shipbuilder or steel fabricator typically dealing in contracts worth millions. Indeed, Jack Brown recalls that, shortly after his businesses collapsed, he was

telephoned by John Peach, the managing director of the nearby smallish Ferguson's shipyard (part of the nationalised British Shipbuilders) who wished to offer commiserations. Peach told him, 'We lost

RIGHT: The small passenger and vehicle ferry *Eilean Bhearnaraigh* manoeuvres in the James Watt dock basin prior to going on trials. *(Jack Brown collection)*

£6.4 million last year and we're still here. It seems odd that you have gone after such a small loss.'

Looking back, Cargospeed's fate in the early 1980s was a microcosm of the de-industrialisation experienced by Britain as a whole. The company's design and engineering expertise was substantial and the equipment it supplied was of a high quality, yet due to a lack of finance and a grander vision, it was unable to achieve the growth that made its rivals, MacGregor and Navire, the dominant suppliers of hatch covers and ferry vehicle deck equipment. Cargospeed never cracked the important Scandinavian market and remained primarily a manufacturer for British and British Commonwealth ferry and liner companies. Nonetheless, Cargospeed played an important role in the development of roll-on, roll-off ferries and cargo vessels and certain projects – notably

the paper and car carriers *Laurentian Forest* and *Avon Forest* – were outstanding in terms of their design ambition and engineering complexity. While in competition with MacGregor and Navire, Brown felt it was necessary to protect his ideas. Upwards of 40 innovations were patented in the 1958-1981 period, mostly ro-ro related.

Although fabricating equipment for ro-ro vessels incorporating many innovations formed a significant part of Cargospeed's business, the majority of Cargospeed's contracts were for Velle hatch covers and 'Shipshape' cranes. Over 300 Velle cranes were designed and manufactured at Garvel, the largest of which was a 80-tonne duty outfit for the Royal Australian Navy's *Tobruk*. Other 'Shipshape' crane installations deserving mention were the seven *Menelaus* class vessels for Blue Funnel Line (Ocean Transport and Trading); the seven *Brunes* class Kr. Jebsen bulk carriers for

RIGHT: The *Eilean Bhearnaraigh*'s bow ramp system demonstrated on the beach at Largs *(Jack Brown collection)*

which Cargospeed devised an ingenious four-rope grabbing system, and no fewer than 30 of the successful Austin & Pickersgill-built SD14 class general cargo ship.

Equipment was supplied to upwards of 50 shipyards of which 18 were in the UK and others in Argentina, Australia, Belgium, Canada, Denmark, the Irish Republic, France, Germany, Greece, The Netherlands, Hong Kong, Italy, Japan, Norway, Singapore and Sweden. Business trips to visit his clients in these countries involved Brown in a great amount of travel, including lengthy flights to Australia and Canada. Because it was also necessary to supervise activities in Greenock, the duration of such trips was limited to little more than two weeks, but required near round-the-clock working for a fortnight in advance and for another fortnight upon return to catch up.

A major advantage for Cargospeed was Brown's familiarity with all aspects of ship design and construction, and another benefit was the combined design and manufacture of equipment 'in-house' which allowed problem-solving on the spot. Brown's daily routine included observing progress with plans in the drawing office, and keeping a watchful eye on manufacturing progress in the George Brown & Co. yard. He

reflects with a lot of satisfaction on the good labour relations enjoyed with yard workers and with office staff.

Despite the fact that hatch cover and 'Shipshape' crane contracts formed the bulk of Cargospeed's regular turnover, it was Brown's designs for vehicle deck equipment for installation on roll-on, roll-off ferries that are his proudest achievement. On the world's busiest ferry routes across the Dover Strait, the number of freight vehicles carried rose from 21,377 in 1967 to 691,537 in 1983 – a growth rate of 24 per cent per annum. This was thanks in no small part to ferries equipped with Cargospeed ro-ro systems. Strong growth continued with Dover handling 2,400,000 freight vehicles in 2014.

More than three decades after Cargospeed was liquidated – several vessels using its equipment remain in service. After a period in lay-up, the former Caledonian MacBrayne Clyde ferry *Saturn* has recently been re-activated for service on the Pentland Firth as the *Orcadia*. In Greece, the *Agios Georgios* (ex-*Hengist*) and *Vitsentzos Kornaros* (ex-*Viking Viscount*) continue in Aegean service. In the Western Mediterranean, the *Moby Love* (ex-*Saint Eloi*) connects the Italian mainland with Elba and the *Sherbatskiy* (ex-*Pride of Free*

RIGHT: B&I's **Leinster** now operates a five hours service between Prince Edward Island and the Magdalen Islands. *(Bruce Peter)*

RIGHT: B&I's **Leinster** now operates a five hours service between Prince Edward Island and the Magdalen Islands. *(Bruce Peter)*

BELOW: The **Express Santorini** (ex **Chartres**) arriving at Paros. She remains in service today with operations in Greece and the Azores. *(Miles Cowsill)*

Enterprise) meanwhile shuttles across the Strait of Gibraltar between Spain and Morocco. Both the former *Connacht* and *Leinster* also continue, the former as Jadrolinija's *Dubrovnik* between Italy and Croatia and the latter as the *Madeleine* between Souris in Quebec and Cap-aux-Meules in the Madeleine Islands in the Gulf of St Lawrence. Other Cargospeed-equipped ferries still exist, for example the former *Iona* and *Horsa*, but these are no longer in regular service and must be presumed shortly bound for scrapping.

Three of the five Cargospeed-equipped naval Royal Fleet Auxiliary ships remain in existence; the former *Lyness* as the American *Texas Clipper III*, while the *Fort Grange* and *Fort Rosalie* (ex-*Fort Austin*) are still in commission with the Royal Navy. Two landing ships also survive, the *Sir Bedivere* as the Brazilian Navy's *Almirante Saboia* and the *Sir Tristram*, which is currently moored at Portland as a British naval training ship. In addition, the formerly civilian car and paper carriers *Laurentian Forest* and *Avon Forest* are now US Military supply ships, named the *Cape Lobos* and *Cape Lambert* respectively. Thus, Cargospeed-designed equipment remains operational on various diverse vessel types and that is surely testimony to its quality and adaptability. Jack Brown can reflect with pride on his remarkable career in shipbuilding.

TOP: The *Agios Georgios* (ex *Hengist*) departs Sifnos in the Eastern Cyclades in the summer of 2014. *(Bruce Peter)*

MIDDLE: In 2014, Cargospeed ro-ro equipment continues in use on a number of vessels. Here, we see the vehicle deck of the Greek-owned *Agios Georgios* (ex *Hengist* of 1972) with her original elevating platform decks still in operation. *(Bruce Peter)*

BELOW: Lanes Lines' Aegean ferry *Vitsentzos Komaros* motors out of Piraeus on a summer evening; originally Townsend Thoresen's *Viking Viscount,* she too retains her original Cargospeed elevating platform deck system. Ferries in Greek domestic service have sealed bow doors and are fitted with more simple stern ramps than the types used when in Channel service from the UK. *(Bruce Peter)*

Appendix 1
Vessels built by George Brown & Co.

Name/date/tonnage/owner

1. Name and particulars not recorded – predates the formation of George Brown & Co. in 1900
2. Name and particulars not recorded – predates the formation of George Brown & Co. in 1900
3. Name and particulars not recorded – predates the formation of George Brown & Co. in 1900
4. Name and particulars not recorded – predates the formation of George Brown & Co. in 1900
5. *Princess Beara* 1901 202gt Steam passenger and cargo ship Bantry Bay Steamship Company, Ireland
6. *Elisa* 1901 138gt Steam cargo ship D. McEwan, Glasgow
7. Name not recorded Steam passenger harbour ferry Bombay Harbour Authority
8. *Yarmouth* 1902 438gt Steam passenger and cargo ship H. Newhouse & Co., Great Yarmouth
9. *Grace* 1902 70gt Steam tug Flower & Everett, London
10. *Eagle* 1902 182gt Steam cargo ship Joseph Rank Ltd, Hull
11. *Lion* 1902 87gt Steam Tug Associated Cement Corporation, London
12. *Tiger* 1902 44gt Steam tug Associated Cement Corporation, London
13. Name not recorded 1902 Steam passenger harbour ferry Bombay Harbour Authority
14. *Maretanza II* 1903 232gt Steam yacht Sir John Denison-Pender, London
15. *Hawthorn* 1903 307gt Steam cargo ship, Boston & Hull Steamship Company, Hull
16. *Carriden* 1903 666gt Steam cargo ship Love & Stewart, Glasgow
17. *Gael* 1903 108gt Steam cargo ship J. May & Co., Glasgow
18. *Juno* 1903 241gt Steam passenger and cargo ship (Gulf Steamship Company) Adelaide Steamship Company, Adelaide
19. *Levant* 1903 283gt Steam cable ship Eastern Telegraph Company, London
20. *Protector* 1903 161gt Steam fishery cruiser Eastern Sea Fisheries Committee, Boston
21. Steel caisson to support dock gate 1904 Brazilian Government, Rio de Janeiro
22. *Tighnamara* 1904 145gt Steam yacht James Allan, Glasgow
23. *Nathaniel Dunlop* 1904 53gt Steam pilot cutter Clyde Pilot Board, Glasgow
24. *Wellpark* 1904 992gt Steam cargo ship J. &. J. Denholm, Greenock
25. *Glenpark* 1904 992gt Steam cargo ship J. &. J. Denholm, Greenock
26. *Lampits* 1904 20gt Steam passenger ferry Lanark Ward Committee, Lanark
27. *Maretanza V* 1905 279gt Steam yacht Sir John Denison-Pender, London
28. *Starling* 1905 212gt Steam cargo ship Steele & Bennie Ltd, Glasgow
29. *Kintail* 1905 421gt Steam cargo ship M. Finlayson & Co., Glasgow
30. *Sea Nymph* 1906 246gt Steam cargo ship East Coast Steamship Company, King's Lynn
31. *Lady Elsie* 1906 93gt Steam passenger and cargo ship Bantry Bay Steamship Company, Ireland
32. *Misrif Sabah* 1906 129gt Steam passenger ship Sheik of Kuwait
33. *Sanidad* 1906 91gt Steam patrol boat Port Authority of Rio de Janeiro
34. *Yelcho* 1906 219gt Steam salvage tug Chilean Government, Santiago
35. Name not recorded 1906 75gt Steam passenger ferry Jones, Burton & Company, Liverpool
36. Name not recorded 1906 75gt Steam passenger ferry Jones, Burton & Company, Liverpool
37. *Bull* 1907 452gt Steam cargo ship Arracan Company Ltd, Bangkok
38. *Zayda* 1907 604gt Steam cargo ship M. Castello, Buenos Aires
39. Name not recorded 1907 144gt Steam cargo ship M. Castello, Buenos Aires
40. *Mayflower* 1907 97gt Steam driftnet trawler J. Brown & Co., Lerwick
41. *Commonwealth* 1907 97gt Steam driftnet trawler J. Falconer, Buckie
42. *Roosevelt* 1907 97gt Steam driftnet trawler G.T. Scott, Buckie
43. *Maritana* 1907 97gt Steam driftnet trawler Murray & Reid, Buckie
44. *Clyde* 1907 97gt Steam driftnet trawler R.F. Mackay, Buckie
45. *Karatta* 1907 527gt Steam passenger and cargo ship (Gulf Steamship Company) Adelaide Steamship Company, Adelaide
46. *Lloyd Uruguayo* 1907 627gt Steam cargo ship Lloyd Uruguayo Company, Montevideo
47. *Lady Sybil* 1908 676gt Steam passenger and cargo ship Magdalen Islands Steamship Company, Canada
48. *Presidente* 1908 146gt Steam turbine passenger ship Brazilian Railway Company, Rio de Janeiro
49. *Ludovico* 1908 650gt Steam turbine coastal cargo ship T. Deposito, Buenos Aires
50. *Ardnagrena* 1908 223gt Steam cargo ship J. Waterson, Belfast
51. *Mercedes III* 1908 98gt Steam tug S. J. Price & Company, Cardiff
52. *Lintie* 1909 172gt Steam cargo ship Steele & Bennie Ltd, Glasgow
53. *Alyn* 1909 350gt Steam cargo ship Hamilton Steamship Company Liverpool
54. *Ostara* 1909 30gt Steam passenger ferry Rio de Janeiro Harbour Company
55. *Duncannon* 1909 141gt Steam passenger and cargo ship Waterford Steamship Company, Waterford
56. *Cassiopeia* 1909 411gt Steam cargo ship F. Vidulich, Trieste
57. *Moy* 1909 88gt Steam grab dredger River Moy Commissioners, Ireland
58. *Aungdipa* 1910 110gt Steam turbine passenger ferry Moulmein River Service, Burma
59. *Aungmala* 1910 110gt Steam turbine passenger ferry Moulmein River Service, Burma
60. *Aungmingala* 1910 110gt Steam turbine passenger ferry Moulmein River Service, Burma
61. *Owenaminane* 1910 402gt Steam grab dredger Cork Harbour Commissioners, Cork
62. *Glenelg* 1910 32gt Steam yacht P. Lang, Greenock
63. Name not recorded 1910 110gt Steam turbine passenger ferry Marshall Cotterel, Melbourne
64. Name not recorded 1910 110gt Steam turbine passenger ferry Marshall Cotterel, Melbourne

65. Name not recorded 1910 98gt Steam tug John Reid & Co., Canada
66. *George Watts* 1911 436gt Steam cargo ship African Association Ltd, Liverpool
67. Name not recorded 1911 35gt Steam passenger ferry Jones, Burton & Company, Liverpool
68. *Dusit* 1911 480gt Steam turbine coastal cargo ship Luang Chit & Co., Bangkok
69. *Lampo* 1911 166gt Steam passenger ship Società di Navigation Vapore La Veloce, Trieste
70. *Lord Bacon* 1911 335gt Steam cargo ship John Bacon Ltd, Liverpool
71. *Lady Bacon* 1911 335gt Steam cargo ship John Bacon Ltd, Liverpool
72. *Artigas* 1911 652gt Steam turbine coastal cargo ship E.J. Vidal & Company, Montevideo
73. *Kopoola* 1911 293gt Steam cargo ship (Gulf Steamship Company) Adelaide Steamship Company, Adelaide
74. *S. W. Scutari* 1911 217gt Steam paddle passenger and cargo ship Austrian Lloyd, Trieste
75. *Zeila* 1912 387gt Steam cargo ship A. W. Savage Ltd, Liverpool
76. *Aurelie G.* 1912 137gt Steam tug McNaughten Line Ltd, Canada
77. Name not recorded 1912 42gt Steam tug John Reid & Company, Canada
78. Name not recorded 1912 42gt Steam tug John Reid & Company, Canada
79. Name not recorded 1912 42gt Steam tug John Reid & Company, Canada
80. *George W. Yates* 1913 111gt Steam tug Canadian Government, Canada
81. *Sir Walter Bacon* 1913 918gt Steam cargo ship John Bacon Ltd, Liverpool
82. *Campista* 1913 1,216gt Steam cargo ship Compania Navegaças, Rio de Janeiro
83. *Ardgarth* 1913 770gt Steam cargo ship Lang & Fulton Ltd, Greenock
84. *Ardglass* 1914 770gt Steam cargo ship Lang & Fulton Ltd, Greenock
85. *Ardgour* 1914 770gt Steam cargo ship Lang & Fulton Ltd, Greenock
86. *Kingfisher* 1914 289gt Steam cargo ship General Steam Navigation Company, London
87. *A43* 1914 34gt Steam tug H.M. Government War Office
88. *Ustaritz* 1914 1,217gt Steam cargo ship Plisson & Company, Paris
89. *Espletto* 1914 1,212gt Steam cargo ship Plisson & Company, Paris
90. *Bissau* 1914 77gt Steam tug African owner not recorded
91. *Amiral* 1914 235gt Steam cargo ship J. Ferreira de Amiral Ltd, Lisbon
92. *Porto Grande* 1915 199gt Steam fresh water tanker St Vincent Water Company, St Vincent
93. *X180* 1915 140gt Motor barge H.M. Admiralty
94. *X179* 1915 140gt Motor barge H.M. Admiralty
95. *Alsace* 1916 120gt Steam passenger and cargo ship Compagnie de Bateau à Vapeur, Guadeloupe
96. *HS62* 1916 48gt Steam tug H.M. Government War Office
97. *Epsom* 1916 820gt Steam paddle minesweeper H.M. Admiralty
98. *X205* 1916 130gt Motor barge H.M. Admiralty
99. *X206* 1916 130gt Motor barge H.M. Admiralty

100. *PT1* 1917 Steam paddle tug H.M. Government War Office
101. *PT2* 1917 Steam paddle tug H.M. Government War Office
102. *Calcium* 1918 613gt Steam cargo ship United Alkali Company Ltd, Liverpool
103. *S51* 1918 293gt Steam paddle river cargo ship H.M. Government War Office
104. *S52* 1918 293gt Steam paddle river cargo ship H.M. Government War Office
105. *James Chapman* 1918 280gt Steam trawler H.M. Admiralty
106. *John Campbell* 1918 280gt Steam trawler H.M. Admiralty
107. *Joseph Connell* 1918 280gt Steam trawler H.M. Admiralty
108. *James Campbell* 1918 280gt Steam trawler H.M. Admiralty
109. *Michael Ging* 1918 280gt Steam trawler H.M. Admiralty
110. *Joseph Gordon* 1918 280gt Steam trawler H.M. Admiralty
111. *Joseph Geddice* 1918 280gt Steam trawler H.M. Admiralty
112. *George Greenfield* 1918 280gt Steam trawler H.M. Admiralty
113. *William Griffiths* 1918 280gt Steam trawler H.M. Admiralty
114. *John Gregory* 1918 280gt Steam trawler H.M. Admiralty
115. *George Graves* 1919 280gt Steam trawler H.M. Admiralty
116. *Samuel Green* 1919 280gt Steam trawler H.M. Admiralty
117. *Kilberry* 1919 630gt Patrol gun boat H.M. Admiralty
118. *Kilbeggan* 1919 630gt Patrol gun boat H.M. Admiralty
119. *Kilbirnie* 1919 630gt Patrol gun boat H.M. Admiralty
120. *Kilbracken* 1919 630gt Patrol gun boat H.M. Admiralty
121. *Peter Carey* 1919 280gt Steam trawler H.M. Admiralty
122. *Daniel Clowden* 1919 280gt Steam trawler H.M. Admiralty
123. Order cancelled
124. Order cancelled
125. Order cancelled
126. Order cancelled
127. Order cancelled
128. Order cancelled
129. Order cancelled
130. Order cancelled
131. *Jomaas* 1920 1,437gt Steam cargo ship Agdesidens Rederi, Arendal
132. *Ada* 1921 2,456gt Steam cargo ship K. Salveson, Kragerø
133. *Albonic* 1921 2,468gt Steam cargo ship W. H. Cockerline, Hull
134. *Garryowen II* 1921 468gt Grain elevator J. Bannatyne & Son, Limerick
135. *Magheramorne* 1921 120gt Grab dredger B.P. Cement Association, Magheramorne
136. *Terneuzen* 1922 704gt Steam cargo ship A.C. Lensen, Terneuzen
137. *Americano* 1922 704gt Steam passenger and cargo ship S.A. Importadora de la Patagonia, Buenos Aires

138. *M.L. Gillespie* 1923 11gt Steam launch R. Pettersen
139. *Albionic* 1924 2,468gt Steam cargo ship W.H. Cockerline & Co., Hull
140. *Evita* 1924 72gt Motor yacht Colonel Gascoigne, Aberford
141. *Agility* 1924 522gt Steam oil tanker F.T. Everard & Sons Ltd, London
142. *Rengam* 1924 185gt Motor passenger and cargo ship Straits Steamship Company, Penang, Malaysia
143. *Dr Gondim* 1924 431gt Steam water tanker Minister Marinha, Rio de Janeiro, Brazil
144. *Rompin* 1924 189gt Motor passenger and cargo ship Straits Steamship Company, Penang, Malaysia
145. *Kooraka* 1925 300gt Motor passenger and cargo ship Adelaide Steamship Company, Adelaide, Australia
146. *Ampang* 1925 213gt Steam passenger and cargo ship Straits Steamship Company, Penang, Malaysia
147. *Gemas* 1925 207gt Steam passenger and cargo ship Straits Steamship Company, Penang, Malaysia
148. *Ceraco* 1925 78gt Steam tug Montreal Heat, Light & Power Company, Montreal, Canada
149. *Audacity* 1925 589gt Steam oil tanker F.T. Everard & Sons Ltd, London
150. *W.F. Vint* 1925 28gt Steam turbine river ferry Ferries Committee, Sunderland Corporation
151. *Paraguasei* 1926 90gt Steam turbine passenger and cargo ship Cia de Navegação Bahia, Bahia, Brazil
152. *Enid* 1926 21gt Motor tug T.B.F. Davis, South Africa
153. *Alice* 1926 90gt Motor yacht Sir Richard Cooper, London
154. *Prowess* 1926 207gt Motor oil tanker F.T. Everard & Sons Ltd, London
155. *Katoora* 1927 327gt Motor coastal cargo ship Adelaide Steamship Company, Adelaide, Australia
156. *Hautaru* 1927 284gt Motor scow Northern Steamship Company, Auckland, New Zealand
157. *Swan* 1927 25gt Steam tug Foreign owner
158. *Name unknown* 1927 Motor barge Foreign owner
159. *Sita* 1927 91gt Steam turbine passenger and cargo ship Bombay Steam Navigation Company, Bombay, India
160. *Jane* 1928 31gt Steam tug Macdonald Stewart Co., Port Swettenham, Malaysia
161. *Authority* 1928 616gt Steam oil tanker F.T. Everard & Sons Ltd, London
162. *A.M.P. 23* 1928 472gt Oil tank barge Anglo Mexican Petroleum Company, London
163. *Craigavad* 1928 38gt Steam tug Belfast Harbour Commissioners, Belfast
164. *Name unknown* 1928 413gt Dumb barge Liebigs Extract of Meat Co., London
165. *Ferry No. 4* 1928 16gt Steam ferry Clyde Navigation Trust, Glasgow
166. *British Youth* 1929 45gt Motor oil tank barge British Petroleum Co. Ltd, London
167. *Charles Clarke* 1929 82gt Steam tug Barranquilla Railway & Pier Company Ltd, London
168. *Name unknown* 1929 150gt Dumb barge Barranquilla Railway & Pier Company Ltd, London
169. *Name unknown* 1929 150gt Dumb barge Barranquilla Railway & Pier Company Ltd, London
170. *Asperity* 1929 699gt Steam oil tanker F.T. Everard & Sons Ltd, London
171. *Penhir* 1930 1,147gt Steam cargo ship Compagnie de Navigation à Vapeur, Nantes, France
172. *Traverse* 1930 317gt Motor salvage ship Quebec Salvage and Wrecking Company, Montreal, Canada
173. *Sealight* 1930 154gt Steam lighter Ross & Marshall, Greenock
174. *Assiduity* 1930 350gt Motor coastal cargo ship F.T. Everard & Sons Ltd, London
175. *Zweena* 1930 640gt Motor coastal oil tanker Anglo-Saxon Petroleum Company, London
176. *Turaqqi* 1930 388gt Steam coastal cargo ship British Tanker Company Ltd, London
177. *Salimeh* 1930 174gt Motor oil barge British Tanker Company Ltd, London
178. *Safiyeh* 1930 174gt Motor oil barge British Tanker Company Ltd, London
179. *Swift de la Plata No. 9* 1931 300gt Motor cattle barge Swift & Co., London
180. *Gebel Ataqa* 1931 397gt Steam oil tanker Anglo-Saxon Petroleum Company, London
181. *Activity* 1931 358gt Motor coastal cargo ship F.T. Everard & Sons Ltd, London
182. *Acclivity* 1931 389gt Motor oil tanker F.T. Everard & Sons Ltd, London
183. *Actuosity* 1933 359gt Motor coastal cargo ship F.T. Everard & Sons Ltd, London
184. *Apricity* 1933 402gt Motor coastal cargo ship F.T. Everard & Sons Ltd, London
185. *Acrity* 1934 403gt Motor coastal cargo ship F.T. Everard & Sons Ltd, London
186. *Shellbrit* 1934 460gt Motor oil tanker Shellmex & British Petroleum Ltd, London
187. *Angularity* 1934 501gt Motor coastal cargo ship F.T. Everard & Sons Ltd, London
188. *Grit* 1934 501gt Motor coastal cargo ship F.T. Everard & Sons Ltd, London
189. *Aseity* 1935 416gt Motor coastal cargo ship F.T. Everard & Sons Ltd, London
190. *Accruity* 1935 456gt Motor coastal cargo ship F.T. Everard & Sons Ltd, London
191. *Giroflee* 1935 Motor yacht R.T.S. Maltby, Dover
192. *Arduity* 1935 304gt Motor coastal cargo ship F.T. Everard & Sons Ltd, London
193. *Curlew* 1935 28gt Steam tug T.A. Findlay & Co., Bombay, India
194. *Anonity* 1936 303gt Motor coastal cargo ship F.T. Everard & Sons Ltd, London
195. *Sagacity* 1936 490gt Motor coastal cargo ship F.T. Everard & Sons Ltd, London
196. *Sedulity* 1936 490gt Motor coastal cargo ship F.T. Everard & Sons Ltd, London
197. *Sincerity* 1936 634gt Motor coastal cargo ship F.T. Everard & Sons Ltd, London
198. *Suavity* 1937 634gt Motor coastal cargo ship F.T. Everard & Sons Ltd, London
199. *Cumbrae* 1937 101gt Motor pilot cutter Clyde Pilot Board, Glasgow
200. Order cancelled
201. *Serenity* 1937 487gt Motor coastal cargo ship F.T. Everard & Sons Ltd, London
202. *Signality* 1937 487gt Motor coastal cargo ship F.T. Everard & Sons Ltd, London
203. *Rinansey* 1938 82gt Motor yacht John Ross, Aberdeen
204. *Edenwood* 1938 1,167gt Motor coastal cargo ship Constantine Steamship Company, Middlesbrough
205. *Sulaf* 1938 37gt Motor tug British Tanker Company, London

206. *Sinjar* 1938 37gt Motor tug British Tanker Company, London

207. *Africa Shell* 1939 706gt Motor coastal oil tanker The Shell Company of East Africa, London

208. *El Nawras* 1939 323gt Motor coastal oil tanker Anglo-Saxon Petroleum Company, London

209. *Aptity* 1939 434gt Motor coastal cargo ship F.T. Everard & Sons Ltd, London

210. *Summity* 1939 554gt Motor coastal cargo ship F.T. Everard & Sons Ltd, London

211. *Supremity* 1939 554gt Motor coastal cargo ship F.T. Everard & Sons Ltd, London

212. *Barbosa* 1939 193gt Steam survey ship Anglo-Saxon Petroleum Company, London

213. *Serenity* 1941 557gt Motor coastal cargo ship F.T. Everard & Sons Ltd, London

214. HMS *Asphodel* 1941 Steam corvette H.M. Royal Navy

215. HMS *Aubrietia* 1941 Steam corvette H.M. Royal Navy

216. HMS *Auricula* 1941 Steam corvette H.M. Royal Navy

217. *Empire Ruby* 1941 677gt Motor oil tanker Elder Dempster & Co., Liverpool

218. HMS *Alyssum* 1941 Steam corvette H.M. Royal Navy

219. HMS *Bellwort* 1941 Steam corvette H.M. Royal Navy

220. HMS *Borage* 1942 Steam corvette H.M. Royal Navy

221. *Empire Dweller* 1942 677gt Motor oil tanker F.T. Everard & Sons Ltd, London

222. HMS *Balsam* 1942 Steam corvette H.M. Royal Navy

223. HMS *Damsey* 1942 Steam trawler H.M. Royal Navy

224. HMS *Chelmer* 1943 Steam turbine frigate H.M. Royal Navy

225. *Empire Audrey* 1943 656gt Motor oil tanker F.T. Everard & Sons Ltd, London

226. HMS *Cam* 1944 Steam turbine frigate H.M. Royal Navy

227. HMS *Arabis* 1944 Steam corvette H.M. Royal Navy

228. HMS *Arbutus* 1944 Steam corvette H.M. Royal Navy

229. HMS *Alnwick Castle* 1944 Steam corvette H.M. Royal Navy

230. *Empire Shelter* 1945 1,333gt Steam rescue ship H.M. Royal Navy

231. Order cancelled

232. *Empire Balham* 1945 1,063gt Motor coastal cargo ship British Channel Islands Shipping Company, London

233. *Empire Bromley* 1945 1,058gt Motor coastal cargo ship James Kelly Ltd, Belfast

234. *Empire Lewisham* 1946 1,059gt Motor coastal cargo ship H.M. Ministry of War Transport Merchant Shipbuilding Department, London

235. *The Emperor* 1946 1958gt Steam coastal cargo ship, J. Hay & Sons Ltd, Glasgow

236. *Empire Lola* 1946 295gt Steam tug H.M. Ministry of War Transport Merchant Shipbuilding Department, London

237. *Shellcoven 3* 30gt 1946gt Motor tug Shellmex & British Petroleum Ltd, London

238. *Shellcoven 4* 30gt 1946gt Motor tug Shellmex & British Petroleum Ltd, London

239. *Socai* 30gt 1946 30gt Motor tug Shellmex & British Petroleum Ltd, London

240. *Soebanjam* 1946 30gt Motor tug Shellmex & British Petroleum Ltd, London

241. *Teddy* 1947 789gt Motor coastal cargo ship Hans Svenningsen, Copenhagen, Denmark

242. *Herdubreid* 1947 266gt Motor refrigerated fish carrier Government of Iceland, Reykjavik

243. *Skjaldbreid* 1948 266gt Motor refrigerated fish carrier Government of Iceland, Reykjavik

244. *Jakob Kjode* 1948 1,759gt Steam cargo ship Inger Jacob Kjode Rederi, Bergen, Norway

245. *Kong Dag* 1948 1,229gt Motor cargo ship Det Sordenfjelske Dampskips-Selskap, Oslo, Norway

246. *Lena* 1948 50gt Steam tug Unknown South American owner

247. *Beauly Firth* 1949 533gt Motor coastal cargo ship Firth Shipping (G.T. Gillie and Blair), Newcastle

248. *Mount Blair* 1949 533gt Motor coastal cargo ship Firth Shipping (G.T. Gillie and Blair), Newcastle

249. *Atonality* 1950 1,221gt Motor oil tanker F.T. Everard & Sons Ltd, London

250. *Iberian Coast* 1950 1,220gt Motor coastal cargo ship Tyne Tees Steam Shipping Co. Ltd, Newcastle (Coast Lines Ltd, Liverpool)

251. *Lenahan* 1950 22gt Motor tug Trans-Arabian Pipeline Corporation, New York

252. *Chandler* 1950 22gt Motor tug Trans-Arabian Pipeline Corporation, New York

253. *Portland* 1951 1,105gt Motor bulk cement ship A/S Dansk Cement, Aalborg, Denmark

254. *Secil Novo* 1951 715gt Motor coastal cargo ship 'Sesil' Cia General de Cal e Cemento, Setubal, Portugal

255. *Ballyhaft* 1952 847gt Steam coastal cargo ship John Kelly Ltd, Belfast

256. *Netherlands Coast* 1953 863gt Motor coastal cargo ship Tyne Tees Steam Shipping Co. Ltd, Newcastle (Coast Lines Ltd, Liverpool)

257. *Ballyhill* 1954 847gt Steam coastal cargo ship John Kelly Ltd, Belfast

258. *Bayad* 1954 452gt Oil bunkering barge Shell Company Ltd, Cairo, Egypt

259. *Sunny* 1954 3,155gt Steam oil tanker A/S Schanches Rederi, Bergen, Norway

260. *Fife Coast* 1954 906gt Motor coastal cargo ship Coast Lines Ltd, Liverpool

261. *Ulster Pioneer* 1955 1,016gt Motor coastal cargo ship Belfast Steamship Company Ltd, Belfast

262. *Brentfield* 1955 1,203gt Motor coastal cargo ship Zillah Shipping Co. Ltd, Liverpool

263. *North Light* 1956 206gt Steam tug Alexandra Towing Company Ltd, London

264. *North Rock* 1956 206gt Steam tug Alexandra Towing Company Ltd, London

265. *Lemana* 1956 946gt Motor coastal cargo ship Wm Holyman & Sons (Pty) Ltd, Launceston, Tasmania

266. *Garnock* 1956 78gt Motor tug Imperial Chemical Industries, London

267. *Parera* 1957 823gt Motor coastal cargo ship Richardson and Co. Ltd, Napier, New Zealand

268. *Otra* 1957 1,325gt Motor coastal cargo ship Christian Salveson & Co. Ltd, Leith

269. *Kingennie* 1958 1,169gt Motor coastal oil tanker Dundee, Perth & London Shipping Company, Dundee

270. *Cantick Head* 1958 1,571gt Motor coastal cargo ship A.F. Henry & MacGregor Ltd, Leith

271. *Siddons* 1959 1,282gt Motor semi-refrigerated cargo ship Lamport & Holt Ltd, Liverpool
272. *Yorkshire Coast* 1959 795gt Motor coastal cargo ship Tyne Tees Steam Shipping Co. Ltd, Newcastle (Coast Lines Ltd, Liverpool)
273. *Brigadier* 1961 223gt Motor tug Steele & Bennie Ltd, Glasgow
274. *Kakuluwa* 1962 grab hopper dredger Colombo Port Commission, Government of Ceylon, Colombo
275. *N. A. Comeau* 1962 1,235gt Passenger and vehicle ferry Traverse Matane-Godbout Ltee, Matane, Canada
276. *Kinnaird Head* 1963 1,985gt A.F. Henry & MacGregor Ltd, Leith
277. *Vasabha* 1963 275gt Motor tug Colombo Port Commission, Government of Ceylon, Colombo
278. *Brenlyn* 1977 133gt Fishing trawler hull
279. *Coronella* 1977 133gt Fishing trawler hull
280. Cancelled trawler hull
281. Cancelled trawler hull
282. Cancelled trawler hull
283. *Aries* 1982 146gt Buoy handling ship Government of Mexico, Veracruz
284. *Leo* 1982 146gt Buoy handling ship Government of Mexico, Mazatlan
285. *Eilean Bhearnaraigh* 1982 67gt Passenger and vehicle ferry
286. *Wilton* 1983 345gt Buoy handling ship Tees & Hartlepool Port Authority

Appendix 2

Vessels for which Cargospeed supplied Velle 'Shipshape' cranes

Vessel's name/year of project/builder/tonnage/owner

Booker Vanguard 1963 Burntisland Shipbuilding Ltd, Burntisland 5,417gt Booker Line Ltd, Liverpool
Hofsjökull 1964 Grangemouth Dockyard Co. Ltd, Grangemouth 2,189gt HF Jocklar Reykjavik
Manchester Renown 1964 Smiths Dock Co. Ltd, Middlesbrough 8,083gt Manchester Liners Ltd, Manchester
Manchester City 1964 Smiths Dock Co. Ltd, Middlesbrough 8,144gt Manchester Liners Ltd, Manchester
Halifax City 1964 Burntisland Shipbuilding Ltd, Burntisland 6,533gt Bristol City Line Ltd, Bristol
Cape Rodney 1965 Lithgows Ltd, Greenock 12,104gt Lyle Shipping Co. Ltd, Glasgow
Tenbury 1965 Burntisland Shipbuilding Ltd, Burntisland 8,014gt Houlder Bros & Co. Ltd
Manchester Commerce (1963) 1966 rebuilding by Smiths Dock Co. Ltd, Middlesbrough 8,167gt Manchester Liners Ltd, Manchester
Cape St Vincent 1966 John Brown & Co. Ltd, Clydebank 12,835gt Lyle Shipping Co. Ltd, Glasgow
YC 1368 1966 rebuilding by George Brown & Co. Ltd, Greenock United States Navy
Booker Viking 1967 Frederiksstad Mekaniska Verkstad, Frederiksstad, Sweden 5,383gt Booker Line Ltd, Liverpool
Vennacher 1967 rebuilding by Eriksbergs Mekaniska Verkstad, Gothenburg Harrisons (Clyde) Ltd, Glasgow
British Monarch (1954) 1968 rebuilding by Eriksbergs Mekaniska Verkstad, Gothenburg Harrisons (Clyde) Ltd, Glasgow
Welsh City 1968 Fairfield Shipbuilding and Engineering, Glasgow 10,790gt Reardon Smith & Co. Ltd, Cardiff
Bencruachan 1968 Charles Connell & Co. Ltd 12,892gt Ben Line (William Thomson & Co. Ltd), Edinburgh
Benstac 1968 Charles Connell & Co. Ltd 12,011gt Ben Line (William Thomson & Co. Ltd), Edinburgh
Cornish City 1969 Fairfield Shipbuilding and Engineering, Glasgow 10,799gt Reardon Smith & Co. Ltd, Cardiff
Helene 1969 Austin & Pickersgill Ltd, Sunderland 14,766gt Counties Ship Management (Kulukundis & Rethymnis), London
Brunes 1969 Lithgows Ltd, Port Glasgow 13,125gt Kr. Jebsens Rederi A/S, Bergen
Baugnes 1969 Lithgows Ltd, Port Glasgow 13,125gt Kr. Jebsens Rederi A/S, Bergen
Aquila 1970 Lithgows Ltd, Port Glasgow 13,125gt Kr. Jebsens Rederi A/S, Bergen
Baknes 1970 Lithgows Ltd, Port Glasgow 13,125gt Kr. Jebsens Rederi A/S, Bergen
Bulknes 1970 Lithgows Ltd, Port Glasgow 13,225gt Kr. Jebsens Rederi A/S, Bergen
County Clare 1970 Austin & Pickersgill Ltd, Sunderland 16,458gt Counties Ship Management (Kulukundis & Rethymnis), London
Brooknes 1970 Lithgows Ltd, Port Glasgow 13,200gt Kr. Jebsens Rederi A/S, Bergen
Binsnes 1970 Lithgows Ltd, Port Glasgow 13,240gt Kr. Jebsens Rederi A/S, Bergen
Granuaile 1970 Ferguson Bros Ltd, Port Glasgow 2003gt Commissioners of the Northern Lights
Benlawers 1970 Upper Clyde Shipbuilders Ltd 12,784gt Ben Line (William Thomson & Co. Ltd), Edinburgh
Sugar Transporter 1970 Lithgows Ltd, Port Glasgow 13,907gt Sugar Line (Tate & Lyle Ltd) London
St François 1970 Bartram & Sons Ltd, Sunderland 9,126gt Denis Freres et Cie, Paris
Sugar Refiner 1970 Lithgows Ltd, Port Glasgow 13,907gt Sugar Line (Tate & Lyle Ltd) London
St Paul 1970 Bartram & Sons Ltd, Sunderland 9,126gt Denis Freres et Cie, Paris
Armadale 1970 Austin & Pickersgill Ltd, Sunderland *10,328gt* Trinder, Anderson & Company Ltd, London
Blidnes 1971 Lithgows Ltd, Port Glasgow 13,116gt Kr. Jebsens Rederi A/S, Bergen
Ramon de Larrinaga 1972 Austin & Pickersgill Ltd, Sunderland 9,181gt Larrinaga Steamship Co., Liverpool
Orbita 1972 Cammell Laird & Co. Ltd, Birkenhead 10,871gt Pacific Steam Navigation Co. Ltd, London
Orduna 1973 Cammell Laird & Co. Ltd, Birkenhead 12,309gt Pacific Steam Navigation Co. Ltd, London
Ortega 1973 Cammell Laird & Co. Ltd, Birkenhead 12,704gt Pacific Steam Navigation Co. Ltd, London
Transvaal 1973 Austin & Pickersgill Ltd, Sunderland 9,089gt Matheson & Co., London
Wambira 1973 rebuilding by Taikoo Dockyard and Engineering Co., Hong Kong State Shipping Service, Freemantle
Beroona 1973 rebuilding by Taikoo Dockyard and Engineering Co., Hong Kong State Shipping Service, Freemantle
Nyanda 1973 Rebuilding by Taikoo Dockyard and Engineering Co., Hong Kong State Shipping Service, Freemantle
Boogala 1974 Rebuilding by Taikoo Dockyard and Engineering Co., Hong Kong State Shipping Service,

Freemantle

Strathdevon 1974 Austin & Pickersgill Ltd, Sunderland
9,214gt Peninsular & Oriental Steam Navigation
Company, London

Strathdare 1975 Austin & Pickersgill Ltd, Sunderland
9,214gt Peninsular & Oriental Steam Navigation
Company, London

Strathdirk 1975 Austin & Pickersgill Ltd, Sunderland
9,214gt Peninsular & Oriental Steam Navigation
Company, London

Westland 1975 Austin & Pickersgill Ltd, Sunderland
8,929gt Koninklijke Nederlandsche Stoomboot-
Maatschappij, Amsterdam

Strathdoon 1976 Austin & Pickersgill Ltd, Sunderland
9,230gt Peninsular & Oriental Steam Navigation
Company, London

Strathduns 1976 Austin & Pickersgill Ltd, Sunderland
9,230gt Peninsular & Oriental Steam Navigation
Company, London

Ajana 1976 Austin & Pickersgill Ltd, Sunderland 9,006gt
Australind Steam Navigation Ltd

Strathdyce 1977 Austin & Pickersgill Ltd, Sunderland
9,230gt Peninsular & Oriental Steam Navigation
Company, London

Atlanta (1959) 1977 rebuild by Western Ship Repairers
Ltd, Liverpool 1,239gt Commissioners of Irish Lights

Salta 1977 Robb Caledon Ltd, Leith 8,922gt Empresa
Lineas Maritimas Argentinas SA, Buenos Aires

July 2 1977 Robb Caledon Ltd, Leith 8,922gt Empresa
Lineas Maritimas Argentinas SA, Buenos Aires

Menelaus 1977 Mitsubishi Heavy Industries, Nagasaki
17,180gt Blue Funnel Line (Ocean Transport &
Trading Ltd)

Memnon 1977 Mitsubishi Heavy Industries, Nagasaki
17,180gt Blue Funnel Line (Ocean Transport &
Trading Ltd)

Melampus 1977 Mitsubishi Heavy Industries, Nagasaki
17,180gt Blue Funnel Line (Ocean Transport &
Trading Ltd)

Menestheus 1977 Mitsubishi Heavy Industries, Nagasaki
17,146gt Blue Funnel Line (Ocean Transport &
Trading Ltd)

Tucuman 1978 Robb Caledon Ltd, Leith 8,922gt
Empresa Lineas Maritimas Argentinas SA, Buenos
Aires

Almirante Storni 1978 Enselada Shipyard Buenos Aires
8,922gt Empresa Lineas Maritimas Argentinas SA,
Buenos Aires

Cluden 1978 Austin & Pickersgill Ltd, Sunderland
9,327gt Matheson & Co., London

RFA *Fort Grange* 1978 Scott's Shipbuilding, Greenock
20,043gt H.M. Government Ministry of Defence

RFA *Fort Austin* 1979 Scott's Shipbuilding, Greenock
20,043gt H.M. Government Ministry of Defence

Nequen 2 1979 Enselada Shipyard Buenos Aires
8,922gt Empresa Lineas Maritimas Argentinas SA,
Buenos Aires

Libertador General Jose de San Martin 1979 Enselada
Shipyard Buenos Aires 8,922gt Empresa Lineas
Maritimas Argentinas SA, Buenos Aires

Bronte 1979 Austin & Pickersgill Ltd, Sunderland
9,324gt Lamport & Holt Ltd, Liverpool

Browning 1979 Austin & Pickersgill Ltd, Sunderland
9,324gt Lamport & Holt Ltd, Liverpool

Boswell 1979 Austin & Pickersgill Ltd, Sunderland
9,324gt Lamport & Holt Ltd, Liverpool

Belloc 1980 Austin & Pickersgill Ltd, Sunderland 9,099gt
Lamport & Holt Ltd, Liverpool

Roachbank 1979 Sunderland Shipbuilders Ltd 11,452gt
Bank Line (Andrew Weir Shipping Ltd), London

Ruddbank 1979 Sunderland Shipbuilders Ltd 12,214gt
Bank Line (Andrew Weir Shipping Ltd), London

Troutbank 1979 Sunderland Shipbuilders Ltd 11,452gt
Bank Line (Andrew Weir Shipping Ltd), London

Pikebank 1979 Sunderland Shipbuilders Ltd 12,214gt
Bank Line (Andrew Weir Shipping Ltd), London

Dacebank 1979 Sunderland Shipbuilders Ltd 12,214gt
Bank Line (Andrew Weir Shipping Ltd), London

Tenchbank 1979 Sunderland Shipbuilders Ltd 12,214gt
Bank Line (Andrew Weir Shipping Ltd), London

Badagry Palm 1979 Sunderland Shipbuilders Ltd
12,025gt Palm Line (Ocean Transport & Trading Ltd),
Liverpool

Dr Atilio Malvagni 1980 Enselada Shipyard Buenos Aires
8,922gt Empresa Lineas Maritimas Argentinas SA,
Buenos Aires

Presidente Ramon S. Castillo 1980 Enselada Shipyard
Buenos Aires 8,922gt Empresa Lineas Maritimas
Argentinas SA, Buenos Aires

Maron 1980 Scott Lithgow Ltd, Greenock 16,482gt Blue
Funnel Line (Ocean Transport & Trading Ltd),
Liverpool

Mentor 1980 Scott Lithgow Ltd, Greenock 16,482gt
Blue Funnel Line (Ocean Transport & Trading Ltd),
Liverpool

Myrmidon 1980 Scott Lithgow Ltd, Greenock 16,482gt
Blue Funnel Line (Ocean Transport & Trading Ltd),
Liverpool

HMAS *Tobruk* Carrington Slipways Pty Ltd Royal
Australian Navy

General Manuel Belgrano 1981 Enselada Shipyard
Buenos Aires 8,922gt Empresa Lineas Maritimas
Argentinas SA, Buenos Aires

Murree 1981 Austin & Pickersgill Ltd, Sunderland
11,940gt Pakistan National Line

Kagnan 1981 Austin & Pickersgill Ltd, Sunderland
11,940gt Pakistan National Line

Ayubia 1981 Austin & Pickersgill Ltd, Sunderland
11,940gt Pakistan National Line

Appendix 3
Cargospeed and Cargospeed/Velle Hatch Covers

Vessel's name/year of project/builder/tonnage/owner

Middlesex Trader 1963 Austin & Pickersgill Ltd,
Sunderland 13,581gt Trader Navigation Co. Ltd

Hofsjökull 1964 Grangemouth Dockyard Co. Ltd,
Grangemouth 2,189gt HF Jocklar, Reykjavik

Surrey Trader 1964 Austin & Pickersgill Ltd, Sunderland
13,203gt Trader Navigation Co. Ltd

St Finbarr 1964 Ferguson Bros Ltd, Port Glasgow
1,139gt Thomas Hamling & Co. Ltd

Ardgarvel 1965 James Lamont & Co. Ltd, Port Glasgow
1,121gt P MacCallum & Sons Ltd

Elysia 1965 Hawthorn Leslie Ltd, Newcastle 8,531gt
Anchor Line Ltd, Glasgow

Avocet 1965 John Lewis & Sons Ltd, Aberdeen 584gt
General Steam Navigation Co. Ltd, London

Albatross 1965 John Lewis & Sons Ltd, Aberdeen 584gt
General Steam Navigation Co. Ltd, London

Sicilia 1965 Bartram & Sons Ltd, Sunderland 6,120gt
Anchor Line Ltd, Glasgow

Tenbury 1965 Burntisland Shipbuilding Ltd, Burntisland

8,014gt Houlder Bros & Co. Ltd

Baron Inverforth 1965 Austin & Pickersgill Ltd, Sunderland 17,238gt H Hogarth & Co. Ltd, Glasgow

Terrier 1965 Rebuilding by George Brown & Co. Ltd, Greenock Coast Lines Ltd

Ranger Ajax 1965 Brooke Marine Ltd, Lowestoft 778gt G.R. Purdy Ltd (Ranger Fishing Co. Ltd)

Ranger Apollo 1965 Brooke Marine Ltd, Lowestoft 778gt G.R. Purdy Ltd (Ranger Fishing Co. Ltd)

Ranger Aurora 1966 Brooke Marine Ltd, Lowestoft 778gt G.R. Purdy Ltd (Ranger Fishing Co. Ltd)

Lairdsfox (1952) 1966 rebuilt Ardrossan Drydock Co. Ltd 562gt Coast Lines Ltd

Lairdsfield (1953) 1966 rebuilt by Manchester Drydocks Ltd 504gt Burns Laird & Co. Ltd

Aberthaw Fisher 1966 Ailsa Shipbuilding Co. Ltd, Troon 2,355gt Austin & Pickersgill Ltd, Sunderland James Fisher & Sons, Barrow in Furness

Kingsnorth Fisher 1966 Hall, Russell & Co. Ltd, Aberdeen 2,330gt James Fisher & Sons, Barrow in Furness

Othello 1966 Yarrow & Co. Ltd, Glasgow 1,573gt Hellyer Bros Ltd (Associated Fisheries)

Cassio 1966 Yarrow & Co. Ltd, Glasgow 1,573gt Hellyer Bros Ltd (Associated Fisheries)

Orisino 1966 Yarrow & Co. Ltd, Glasgow 1,574gt Hellyer Bros Ltd (Associated Fisheries)

Coriolanus 1967 Yarrow & Co. Ltd, Glasgow 1,105gt Hellyer Bros Ltd (Associated Fisheries)

Clydesdale 1967 Scott's Shipbuilding, Greenock 24,024gt Houlder Bros & Co. Ltd

Marlin 1967 Brooke Marine Ltd, Lowestoft 632gt Amalgamated Fisheries Pty Ltd

Redfin 1967 Brooke Marine Ltd, Lowestoft 632gt Amalgamated Fisheries Pty Ltd

St Jason 1967 Ferguson Bros Ltd, Port Glasgow 1,288gt Thomas Hamling & Co. Ltd

Lancashire Coast 1967 rebuild by Harland & Wolff Ltd, Belfast 1,020gt Coast Lines Ltd

Vardefjell 1968 Firth of Clyde Drydock Co. Ltd 11,991gt Olsen & Uglestad A/S

St Jerome 1968 Ferguson Bros Ltd, Port Glasgow 1,288gt Thomas Hamling & Co. Ltd

St Jasper 1968 Ferguson Bros Ltd, Port Glasgow 1,286gt Thomas Hamling & Co. Ltd

Ocean Transport (1962) 1968 rebuild by Alexander Stephen & Sons, Glasgow 8,429gt Houlder Bros & Co. Ltd

Westbury (1960) 1968 rebuild by Alexander Stephen & Sons, Glasgow 8,414gt Houlder Bros & Co. Ltd

Queen Elizabeth 2 1969 John Brown & Co. Ltd, Clydebank 65,683gt Cunard Line Ltd

Volnay 1969 John Brown & Co. Ltd, Clydebank 22,189gt Harrisons (Clyde) Ltd, Glasgow

Ibadan Palm 1969 Rebuilding by Middle Docks & Engineering Ltd, South Shields 5,658gt Palm Line (Ocean Transport & Trading Ltd)

Islander 1969 John Lewis & Sons Ltd, Aberdeen 250gt Orkney Isles Shipping Co. Ltd

C.S. Forrester 1969 Charles D. Holmes, Beverley 185gt Newington Trawlers Ltd

Cirolana 1970 Ferguson Bros Ltd, Port Glasgow 1,919gt H.M. Government Department of Agriculture & Fisheries

Shaftesbury (1958) 1970 rebuild by Upper Clyde Shipbuilders, Glasgow 8,276gt Houlder Bros & Co. Ltd

Tewkesbury (1959) 1970 rebuild by Upper Clyde Shipbuilders, Glasgow 8,532gt Houlder Bros & Co. Ltd

Wicklow 1971 Verolme Cork Dockyard 3,438gt British & Irish Steam Packet Company

Scotia 1971 Ferguson Bros Ltd, Port Glasgow 1,699gt H.M. Government Department of Agriculture & Fisheries (Scotland)

Marinex V 1971 Ferguson Bros Ltd, Port Glasgow 2,825gt Marinex Gravel Ltd, London

Ranger Cadmus 1971 Brooke Marine Ltd, Lowestoft 1,106gt G.R. Purdy Ltd (Ranger Fishing Co. Ltd)

Ranger Calliope 1972 Brooke Marine Ltd, Lowestoft 1,106gt G.R. Purdy Ltd (Ranger Fishing Co. Ltd)

Ranger Callisto 1972 Brooke Marine Ltd, Lowestoft 1,106gt G.R. Purdy Ltd (Ranger Fishing Co. Ltd)

Ranger Castor 1972 Brooke Marine Ltd, Lowestoft 1,106gt G.R. Purdy Ltd (Ranger Fishing Co. Ltd)

St Benedict 1973 Ferguson Bros Ltd, Port Glasgow 1,587gt Thomas Hamling & Co. Ltd

Kilkenny 1973 Verolme Cork Dockyard 1,514gt British & Irish Steam Packet Company

Goth 1974 Ferguson Bros Ltd, Port Glasgow 1,169gt British United Trawlers Ltd

Roman 1974 Ferguson Bros Ltd, Port Glasgow 1,154gt British United Trawlers Ltd

Norse 1974 Scott & Sons (Bowling) Ltd 1,448gt British United Trawlers Ltd

Bass Trader (1961) 1974 rebuild by New South Wales State Dockyard 4,129gt Australian National Line

Appendix 4
Cargospeed door, ramp and/or platform deck systems

Vessel's name/year of completion/client/vessel's gross tonnage/equipment supplied/vessel's owner

N.A. Comeau 1962 George Brown & Co., Greenock 1,235gt Stern door Traverse Matane Godbout

Holyhead Ferry I 1965 Hawthorn, Leslie Ltd, Newcastle 3,879gt Stern vehicle deck door British Rail Shipping

Sieur D'Amours 1966 T. Davie Shipyard Ltd, Lauzon, Quebec, Canada 2,558gt Stern door Traverse Matane Godbout

Seaway Princess 1966 Hong Kong & Whampoa Dockyard Co. 1,109gt Stern door Northern Steamship Company

RFA *Lyness* 1966 Swan Hunter, Wallsend 12,359gt Side superstructure doors H.M. Government Ministry of Defence

RFA *Sir Galahad* 1966 Alexander Stephen & Sons, Glasgow 6,390gt Bow door gear and davits for life rafts H.M. Government Ministry of Defence

RFA *Stromness* 1967 Swan Hunter, Wallsend 12,359gt Side superstructure doors H.M. Government Ministry of Defence

RFA *Tarbatness* 1967 Sawn Hunter, Wallsend 12,359gt Side superstructure doors H.M. Government Ministry of Defence

RFA *Sir Geraint* 1967 Alexander Stephen & Sons, Glasgow 6,390gt Bow door gear and davits for life rafts H.M. Government Ministry of Defence

RFA *Sir Bedivere* 1967 Hawthorn Leslie Ltd, Newcastle 6,390gt Bow door gear and davits for life rafts H.M. Government Ministry of Defence

RFA *Sir Tristram* 1967 Hawthorn Leslie Ltd, Newcastle 6,390gt Bow door gear and davits for life rafts H.M.

Government Ministry of Defence

Antrim Princess 1967 Hawthorn, Leslie Ltd, Newcastle 3,730gt Bow and stern vehicle deck doors and folding platform decks British Rail Shipping

Lion 1967 Cammell Laird Ltd, Birkenhead 3,333gt Bow and stern vehicle deck doors and folding platform decks Burns Laird & Co. Ltd

Lancashire Coast (1954) 1967 Harland & Wolff Ltd, Belfast 1,020gt Rebuilding with car loading ramp Coast Lines Ltd

RFA *Sir Percivale* 1968 Hawthorn Leslie Ltd, Newcastle 6,390gt Bow door gear and davits for life rafts H.M. Government Ministry of Defence

Bencruachan 1968 Charles Connell & Co. Ltd, Glasgow 12,892gt Side shell doors and pallet platforms Ben Line (William Thomson & Co. Ltd)

Benstac 1968 Charles Connell & Co. Ltd, Glasgow 12,011gt Side shell doors and pallet platforms Ben Line (William Thomson & Co. Ltd)

Ibadan Palm (1959) rebuilding date not known (late-1960s) Middle Docks & Engineering Ltd, South Shields 5,658gt Retro-fitting of portable car decks Palm Line (Ocean Transport & Trading Ltd)

Elmina Palm (1957) rebuilding date not known (late-1960s) Smiths Docks Ltd, Middlesbrough 5,356gt Retro-fitting of portable car decks Palm Line (Ocean Transport & Trading Ltd)

Kano Palm (1958) rebuilding date not known (late-1960s) Middle Docks & Engineering Ltd, South Shields 6,012gt Retro-fitting of portable car decks Palm Line (Ocean Transport & Trading Ltd)

Katsina Palm (1957) rebuilding date not known (late-1960s) Middle Docks & Engineering Ltd, South Shields 8,734gt Retro-fitting of portable car decks Palm Line (Ocean Transport & Trading Ltd)

Seal 1968 Stern door H.M. Government Ministry of Defence

Vortigern 1969 Swan Hunter Shipbuilding Ltd, Newcastle 4,797gt Bow and stern vehicle deck doors and elevating platform decks British Rail Shipping

Islander 1969 John Lewis & Sons Ltd, Aberdeen, 'Gullwing' shell/deck doors Orkney Isles Shipping Co. Ltd

John Burke 1970 Adelaide Ship Construction Ltd, Port Adelaide, Australia 1,464gt Stern door John Burke Pty Ltd

Fremantle Star (1960) 1970 rebuilding by Cammell Laird Ltd, Birkenhead 8,403gt Retrofitting of side shell doors and pallet platforms Blue Star Line

Iona 1970 Alisa Shipbuilding Co., Troon 1970 Stern ramp Scottish Transport Group

Ailsa Princess 1971 Cantiere Navale Breda, Marghera, Italy 3,908gt Bow and stern vehicle deck doors and elevating platform decks British Rail Shipping

Mary Holyman 1971 Boele's Scheepswerven en Machinefabriek, Bolnes, the Netherlands 2,577gt Stern ramp, internal ramp and ramp cover William Brandt Leasing Ltd

Glen Sannox (1957) 1971 Alisa Shipbuilding Co., Troon 1,269gt Stern ramp Scottish Transport Group

Caribbean Endeavour 1971 rebuilding 3,740gt extra platform deck and access ramp Co-ordinated Caribbean Transport Co.

Lionheart (1960) 1972 rebuilding 5,904gt A/S Nymo Mek Verksted rebuilding extra platform deck and access ramp Co-ordinated Caribbean Transport Co.

Hengist 1972 Arsenal de la Marine National Francaise, Brest, France 5,596gt Bow and stern doors and elevating platform decks British Rail Shipping

Horsa 1972 Arsenal de la Marine National Francaise, Brest, France 5,596gt Bow and stern doors and elevating platform decks British Rail Shipping

Senlac 1973 Arsenal de la Marine National Francaise, Brest, France 5,131gt Bow and stern doors and elevating platform decks British Rail Shipping

Laurentian Forest 1972 Port Weller Dry Docks Ltd, Ontario, Canada 16,284gt Shell doors, access ramps, internal ramps, lifts and elevating platform decks Burnett Steamship Company Ltd

Avon Forest 1973 Port Weller Dry Docks Ltd, Ontario, Canada 16,382gt Shell doors, access ramps, internal ramps, lifts and elevating platform decks Burnett Steamship Company Ltd

Copenhagen 1974 Vickers Ltd, Barrow 13,758gt Side shell doors K/S Nordline

Chartres 1974 Dubigeon-Normandie SA, Prairie au Duc, Nantes, France 4,590gt Bow and stern doors and elevating platform decks SNCF French Railways

Chi-Cheemaun 1974 Collingwood Shipyards, Ontario, Canada 6,991gt Bow door and stern door Provincial Government of Ontario

St Ola 1974 Hall Russell & Co. Ltd, Aberdeen Bow and stern doors, platform decks and car elevator P&O Short Sea Shipping Ltd

Camille Marcoux 1974 Marine Industrie Ltd, Sorel, Quebec, Canada 6,122gt Bow and stern doors and elevating platform decks Traversiers du Quebec

Jupiter 1974 James Lamont & Co., Port Glasgow 854gt Stern and side ramps Scottish Transport Group

Netley Castle 1974 Ryton Marine Ltd, Wallsend on Tyne 1,858gt Bow and stern ramps and elevating platform decks Red Funnel Steamers Ltd

Pioneer 1974 Robb Caledon Shipbuilders Ltd, Leith 1,071gt Stern ramp Scottish Transport Group

Avalon (1963) 1974 Alexander Stephen & Sons, Glasgow 6,584gt Side shell door British Rail

Saint Eloi 1975 Cantieri Navali di Pietra Ligure, Pietra Ligure, Italy, 4,649gt Bow and stern doors and elevating platform decks Angleterre-Loraine-Alsace de Navegation S.A., Dunkerque, France

Incan St Laurent 1975 Burrard Dry Dock Co. 7,892gt Stern door Incan Ships Ltd, Montreal

Viking Venturer 1975 Aalborg Værft, Denmark 6,387gt Bow and stern vehicle deck doors and elevating platform decks Townsend Thoresen (European Ferries Ltd)

Viking Valiant 1975 Aalborg Værft, Denmark 6,387gt Bow and stern vehicle deck doors and elevating platform decks Townsend Thoresen (European Ferries Ltd)

Dundalk 1975 Verolme Cork Dockyard, Ireland 2,353gt Bow and stern doors British & Irish Steam Packet Company

Juno 1975 James Lamont & Co., Port Glasgow 854gt Stern and side ramps Scottish Transport Group

Prinses Maria Esmeralda 1975 Cockerill Yards, Hoboken, Belgium 5,635gt Side shell doors, bow door, stern door and elevating platform decks Regie voor Maritiem Transport

Prinses Marie-Christine 1975 Cockerill Yards, Hoboken, Belgium 5,635gt Side shell doors, bow door, stern door and elevating platform decks Regie voor Maritiem Transport

European Gateway 1975 Schichau Unterweser AG, Bremerhaven, West Germany 3,335gt Bow and stern vehicle deck doors and superstructure forward door Townsend Thoresen (European Ferries Ltd)

European Trader 1975 Schichau Unterweser AG, Bremerhaven, West Germany 3,335gt Bow and stern vehicle deck doors and superstructure forward door Townsend Thoresen (European Ferries Ltd)

Viking Voyager 1976 Aalborg Værft, Denmark 6,387gt Bow and stern doors and elevating platform decks Townsend Thoresen (European Ferries Ltd)

Viking Viscount 1976 Aalborg Værft, Denmark 6,387gt Bow and stern doors and elevating platform decks Townsend Thoresen (European Ferries Ltd)

Earl Leofric (ex-*Holyhead Ferry I*) 1976 rebuilding Swan Hunter Shiprepairers Tyne Ltd, Hebburn Bow door and elevating platform decks British Rail

European Clearway 1976 Schichau Unterweser AG, Bremerhaven, West Germany 3,335gt Bow and stern doors and superstructure forward door Townsend Thoresen (European Ferries Ltd)

Prins Albert 1978 Cockerill Yards, Hoboken, Belgium 6,707gt Side shell doors, bow door, stern door and elevating platform decks Regie voor Maritiem Transport

Saturn 1978 Ailsa Shipbuilding Co., Troon 851gt Stern and side ramps Scottish Transport Group

Manx Viking (1976) 1978 rebuilding by Edinburgh Independent Drydock Company 3,594gt Hoistable car deck system

Fort Grange 1978 Scott's Shipbuilding, Greenock 20,043gt Side superstructure doors H.M. Government Ministry of Defence

Fort Austin 1979 Scott's Shipbuilding, Greenock 20,043gt Side superstructure doors H.M. Government Ministry of Defence

Connacht 1979 Verolme Cork Dockyards Ltd, Cork, Ireland 6,807gt Bow and stern doors and elevating platform decks British & Irish Steam Packet Company

Chrissi Ammos 1979 rebuilding Argo Shipbuilding & Repairing Co. Ltd Stern Door Windward Shipping

Azzaur 1979 Selco Shipyard, Singapore 275gt Stern and bow ramps Kuwait Ferries

Spirit of Free Enterprise 1980 Schichau Unterweser AG, Bremerhaven, West Germany 7,591gt Bow and stern doors and elevating platform decks Townsend Thoresen (European Ferries Ltd)

Herald of Free Enterprise 1980 Schichau Unterweser AG, Bremerhaven, West Germany 7,591gt Bow and stern doors and elevating platform decks Townsend Thoresen (European Ferries Ltd)

Pride of Free Enterprise 1980 Schichau Unterweser AG, Bremerhaven, West Germany 7,591gt Bow and stern doors and elevating platform decks Townsend Thoresen (European Ferries Ltd)

Lord Warden (1952) 1980 Retrofitting side shell door British Rail

Saint Columba (1977) 1981 Retrofitting stores crane and stores hatch British Rail

Leinster 1981 Verolme Cork Dockyards Ltd, Cork, Ireland 6,807gt Bow and stern doors and elevating platform decks British & Irish Steam Packet Company

Caledonian Princess (1961) 1981 Retrofitting extra platform decks British Rail

Farha (1973) 1981 rebuilding at Perama, Greece 3,206gt

40 tonnes vehicle elevator Adelphi Vergottis Ltd

Bahjah (1973) 1981 rebuilding at Perama, Greece 3,209gt 40 tonnes vehicle elevator Adelphi Vergottis Ltd

Bibliography

Interview with W. James Ayers, formerly Chief Naval Architect of Townsend and Townsend Thoresen, by Bruce Peter at his home in Reigate on 7th February 2010.

Interview with Jack Brown, formerly managing director of George Brown & Co. of Greenock, by Bruce Peter on 15th September 2014.

Interview with Don Ripley, formerly Chief Draughtsman of British Railways' Naval Architecture Department, by Bruce Peter at the home of Ron Cox on 12th May 2002.

Haresnape, Brian, *Sealink*, Ian Allan, London, 1982.

MacArthur, Ian C., *The Caledonian Steam Packet Co. Ltd: An Illustrated History*, T. Stephenson & Sons, Prescot, 1971.

Ripley, Don and Rogan, Tony, *Designing Ships for Sealink*, Ferry Publications, Kilgetty, 1995.

Robins, Nick, *Ferry Powerful: A History of the Modern British Diesel Ferry*, Bernard McCall, Bristol, 2003.

The Motor Ship

'*Antrim Princess* – the first drive-through ferry for British Railways', February 1968, pp492-496.

'*Vortigern* – a 4,760-gross ton multi-purpose ferry for British Rail', September 1969, pp275-279.

'Second drive-through passenger and vehicle ferry for Stranraer-Larne service', August 1971, pp200-203.

'The 5,000 gross ton *Hengist*: first of three French-built cross-Channel ferries', July 1972, pp149-153.

'First Canadian-built ships for U.K. owners', October 1972, p312.

'*Senlac*: British Rail's new ferry for Newhaven-Dieppe service, May 1973, p100.

'First of four new Caledonian MacBrayne ferries', April 1974, p127.

'*Netley Castle* – new Isle of Wight ferry with Aquamaster propulsion units', June 1974, pp397-400.

'Largest Townsend Thoresen triple-screw ferry', June 1975, pp99-101.

'*Spirit of Free Enterprise*', March 1980, pp41-47.

'*Badagry Palm*: A multi-purpose cargo/container liner for West Africa trade', April 1980, pp30-32.

Shipbuilding and Shipping Record

'Pignon tower crane for shipyard', 22nd March 1962, p387.

'*Holyhead Ferry I* – First UK-Republic of Ireland passenger/vehicle ferry', 25th August 1965, pp280-281.

'British Rail's *Vortigern* looks a winner', 8th August 1969, pp13-16.

Shipping World & Shipbuilder

'*Salta*: First in a series of three standard vessels built by specialist shipbuilders Robb Caledon', February 1977, pp207-210.